JULIE AND

Biograp..,

A Memoir from Stage to Screen

Jacob Jon Slyvan Miller

TABLE OF CONTENTS

Chapter 1

Chapter 2

Chapter 3

Chapter 4

Chapter 5

Chapter 6

Chapter 7

Chapter 8

Chapter 9

Chapter 1

The Thames originates as a trickle just above Oxford in a place known in ancient literature as "Isis." By the time it reaches the great university city, the trickle has become a fair river and fordable, and from there it winds its way through the English countryside, changing levels from time to time, spewing through the gates of some exquisitely pretty locks, passing old villages with lovely names like Sonning, Henley, Marlow, Maidenhead, and Bray.

I've always enjoyed inland waterways, water in general, and water sounds—there's song in water. The brooks are gurgling, and the fountains are splashing. Weirs and waterfalls, tumbling and flowing. When I think of my birthplace, Walton-on-Thames, the river comes to mind first and foremost. I adore the smell of the river, as well as its history and serenity. I was aware of its presence since I was a child. Its majesty centered me, calmed me, and provided some peace.

To this day, everytime I travel into England, I look for a view of the river as we descend toward Heathrow. And then I see it: stately, shining, snaking through the meadows, always calming, always serene.

Julia Elizabeth is the name I was given after my two grandmothers. Julia, my mother's mother, was William Henry Ward's eldest daughter. He was a gardener who met my great-grandmother, Julia Emily Hearmon (often referred to as Emily), while working at a huge home in Stratford-upon-Avon. Great-Granny Emily was a "tweeny," a poor unfortunate who gets up even before the servants and lights their fires so that they, in turn, can see to the household's comforts. She was eleven years old when she enlisted.

After a few years, she and Great-Grandpa William married and relocated to Hersham, where their first daughter, Julia Mary Ward, was born in 1887. There would be a nine-year void until the rest of the family arrived at two-year intervals in a futile attempt to conceive a son. Four daughters, generally known as "the girls," were born, each with a highfalutin name, beginning with Wilhelmina Hearmon, followed by Fenella Henrietta, Nona Doris, and finally Kathleen Lavinia. Thankfully, they were all abbreviated to Mina, Fen, Doll, and Kath. Finally, the long-awaited boy arrived—William Henry, reduced to Harry and then Hadge by the time Julia, the eldest, married...In July 1910, she gave birth to my mother, Barbara Ward Morris. This meant that my mother had an uncle who was only a few years her senior and hence had a built-in playmate.

Grandmother Julia appeared to be a sweet little mouse. My aunt told me she was sensitive, shy, and reserved, yet she loved music and sang fairly well. She wants nothing more in life than to care for and adore her children. My grandfather Arthur was said to find this situation oppressive, and her obvious attempts to please upset him.

Barbara Ward Morris, my mother, was born on July 25, 1910. Arthur did the unimaginable and abandoned his regiment five days later. For a time, the small family seemed to vanish into thin air, but two years later, Arthur was identified as being on the army's missing list by a police officer and was arrested, tried, and sentenced to sixty-three days in military prison for desertion. His superiors may have understood that Julia was a new wife with a tiny infant who needed her husband, for petitions were made on his behalf, and Arthur was formally dismissed after only twenty-nine days in prison.

Julia and Arthur started over. They proceeded to Kent, where Arthur joined the newly created Kent coal-mining colony. My aunt Joan was born on June 30, 1915, to them and her husband. Arthur "deserted" again after her birth, this time leaving his family. He suffered from depression, but it's possible that he went to the more lucrative mining area of South Yorkshire to look for new opportunities, because the Morrises moved again not long after, to the pit village of Denaby, where Arthur was hired as a deputy at the local colliery.

Both sisters attended Miss Allport's Preparatory School for Boys and sisters before moving on to the local school in neighboring Old Denaby. My mother was quite popular and incredibly attractive, according to school records. Aunt Joan was more quiet, and she was usually nervous. She was extremely reliant on my mum. Both girls had beautiful auburn hair and alabaster complexions.

He departed Denaby Colliery near the end of 1921, and the family relocated a few miles away to Swinton. Auntie was six years old at the time, and Mum was eleven. My mother became more accomplished at the piano as Arthur became more busy with his poetry, music, and entertaining—and in 1924, at the age of fourteen, she left school to pursue her piano playing full-time with a private tutor, and just a year and a half later, she had passed the London College of Music's senior-level exams.

Granny Julia took my mother and aunt to Hersham in the summer of 1926 to visit her own mother, dear Great-Granny Emily Ward. This appears to have been a bucolic vacation for the girls, during which they learned the joys of the countryside and all that it had to offer in comparison to the mining towns where they lived.

Granny Julia quickly found work as a maid for Mr. Mortimer, who gave her and the children a place to live. Arthur stayed in Swinton, but tragedy struck: his new lifestyle had strained his relationship with his family, and his casual liaisons with women had led to his developing syphilis. He went down to Hersham, and either realizing that she was happier without him than with him, or knowing that he was ailing and needed care, Julia brought him back and the family was reunited for a while. However, Arthur's vitality quickly faded, and he became skinny and lethargic. On November 16, 1928, he was admitted to the Brookwood Sanatorium in Woking. He died in

August of the following year, at the age of forty-three, from "Paralysis of the Insane."

My mother only discussed this time in their lives once, providing me merely the facts. I begged my aunt Joan to write about it later, but she trembled and replied, "Why would I write about something so terrible?" That place, the smell, the people...screaming, insane." She must have been traumatized, given that she was just thirteen at the time, but I got the impression she was also embarrassed and hesitant to share it with me. Syphilis was far from "genteel." The terrible result of Arthur's deeds was that he infected Julia, and she, too, grew ill and died only two years later. In retrospect, it's not unexpected that my mother's grieving was so visible and prolonged.

For the girls, childhood vanished overnight, and the battle for survival started. The early death of their parents altered the course of my mother's career forever, as she became mother as well as sister to Aunt Joan, taking on the role of full-time caregiver and thus cementing what had always been present—their larger-than-life sibling rivalry and total reliance on each other.

Aunt was still in school, and when the generous headmistress realized the girls were struggling to make ends meet, she arranged for a scholarship for Aunt. Other jobs included a period in a local convalescent home chapel, where Mum played the harmonium while Aunt managed the bellows—Mum frequently exhorting Auntie to "Pump harder!" They frequently chuckled at the contrast between their religious pursuits in the morning and their trashy nightclub professions in the evenings.

Aunt was determined to have talent and may make a solid all-rounder despite her late start, particularly in ballet. Aunt received her tuition in exchange for arriving at 10:30 a.m. to tidy up the studio, dust and plump the cushions, attend to the cleanliness of the cloakrooms, wash up, serve tea to guests in the afternoons between classes, and be a general dogsbody. Mum was also scheduled to play two afternoons per week.

My father's childhood was no different. David Wells, his paternal grandpa, had been a coachman for a Lady Tilson of Guildford, Surrey, and then a custodian for the Wesleyan Chapel there. He and his wife, Fanny Loveland Wells, were Middlesex and Surrey natives, respectively.

Fanny's relatives ran Loveland's, a business in Hersham that made deliveries around town with a pony and trap. David Wilfred Wells was Fanny and David's only child. My grandfather, Young David, was a carpenter/joiner. He was one of the first competent carpenters on the City and Guild's list, and builders would hire him around the hamlet. During a difficult period of unemployment, he rode from Hersham to Wales (approximately sixteen hours distant) in search of a job.
Mr. Charles Packham, Dad's maternal grandpa, was an accomplished gardener. His and Elizabeth Packham's six children were Mary, Susan, Charles, Ellen, Caroline, and Elizabeth Packham.

Elizabeth, the youngest, was a kindergarten teacher when she met and married my paternal grandfather, David Wilfred Wells. David and Elizabeth Wells had four children: Frank, the oldest; Ted, my father; Robert (Uncle Bob); and a girl, Elizabeth, but often referred to as Betty.

Frank, I was informed, was a wonderful man and a magnificent craftsman, but he died of meningitis at the age of thirty, and I never met him. Frank, in addition to being a carpenter, was also a teacher, which motivated my father to become a teacher himself. Bob, the third son, was considered the family's "brains" and became the chief of a research team at Hackbridge Electric in Hersham, which manufactured massive transformers.

Betty, the youngest and only daughter, was born with a mental disability. I'm not sure what caused it, although her mother, my Granny Elizabeth Wells, was supposed to have tried to abort her. The child was a huge financial strain on the family. Despite her seeming beauty, she couldn't communicate and was prone to fits and rages. Because of her disruptive nature, my father could never have friends over to the house. She was placed in a home for the handicapped at a young age, but when Granny Wells went to visit her, she was overcome with regret and brought the kid back home. Betty passed away at the age of twenty-seven. Betty, I believe, had a huge influence on my father, forever changing his perceptions of women as somewhat needy and fragile.

Following the 1914-18 war, there was a subsidy system for young people who wanted to buy a home. David, my grandfather, applied for and received a £70 grant. He purchased a site in Pleasant Place, Hersham, and with the help of his sons and some builder friends, he constructed a two-story house he named "Deldene." There were three modest bedrooms upstairs, as well as a living room, scullery, and an outside toilet. The only source of heat was a fireplace, and the one in the living room featured a trivet that swung into or away from the fire and held a kettle for boiling water or cooking. It was next to a cast-iron baking oven, which was also heated by the fire, as I recall. A pump collected water from the copper tank downstairs and carried it to a tub, but the water was only lukewarm. My father and his brothers preferred to bathe in the rivers Mole, Thames, and Wey. They would immerse themselves in the river after slathering themselves in soap.

Dad was a "practical handicrafts teacher," teaching woodworking, metalworking, basic building, engineering, and so on, but he also substituted for other teachers, teaching math, English literature, and grammar. Because the schools were too small to employ a full-time specialist teacher, he spent one day a week at each of them, riding almost 200 miles a week from Hersham to neighboring villages in Surrey. He also conducted evening classes. He used to own a motorcycle, but he sold it to assist my mother and Aunt Joan keep a roof over their heads after their father died.

Part-time and replacement teachers were paid hourly. He received a princely sum of £11 at the end of the 1932 term, which had to endure until the end of the following month—two months in all. He was eventually awarded a full-time position at the Shere school. His students ranged in age from fourteen to sixteen; youngsters old enough to be responsible when handling dangerous equipment, but who, in many cases, were simply country lads with lots of natural teenage hostility. Dad was patient with all of them. As an amateur boxer, he could take on any of them, and he almost had to a couple of times. He entertained them by playing football with them. He had won their respect and was a well-liked teacher.

My mother supplemented their little income by teaching piano and performing. Aunt Joan, who was always present, had founded her own dancing school in Walton in a location that was Miss LeMarchand's Primary School during the day but accommodated her courses in the afternoons and evenings. She, too, contributed to the coffers by moving in with my parents when they rented a modest property called "Threesome"—perhaps so named due to their combined tenancy.

On October 1, 1935, I was born at Rodney House, Walton-on-Thames' maternity hospital.

He introduced us to the wonders of nature throughout our infancy. One of my first memories is him taking me outdoors to see a giant ant's nest that he had discovered while gardening behind a stone.

Dad was not a religious man, and he once told me that if it weren't for the existence of two things: trees—and man's conscience—he wouldn't believe in God at all. He claimed that mankind would perish on this world if trees did not feed, clothe, shelter, and produce oxygen. Without a conscience, man would most likely have never progressed beyond a primordial level.

Dad, on the other hand, loved church music and listened to Sunday services on the BBC radio. He was rather proud of his light, "bathroom baritone" voice. He sang any hymn or song all the way through, his diction impeccable, loving every note and every syllable. Certain songs would frequently appear in his repertoire, like "Has Anyone Seen My Lady as She Went Passing By?" Handel's "Where E'er You Walk" He was also a good whistler.

My fascination with water is most likely inherited from my father, who enjoyed rivers and lakes. Dad loved renting a skiff and bringing my brother and me for a ride on the Thames. He'd carefully explain before we left the shore, "Now listen, both of you. This can easily tip, so keep your weight low when you enter and exit. "Do not get up."

He appeared to be knowledgeable about a wide range of topics. He was fascinated with language, grammar, and mathematics. He enjoyed studying and would sit at his desk, one hand on his brow, poring over the pages. For him, studying was crucial.

He believed that what he did was insignificant. Many students returned in subsequent years to tell him what a difference he'd made in their lives, and every one of us in the family admired his ability to express a feeling of wonder and awe. He regarded all children the same way: we were young minds who needed to be respected and fostered. In retrospect, it's incredible how plainly he communicated to me that I was loved.

Someone once asked me which of my parents I despised the most. It was a provocative and intriguing topic, since it instantly became clear to me who I loved with all my being...and that was my father. My mother was very important to me, and I remember how much I yearned for her when I was younger, but I don't think I ever completely trusted her.

My brother John was born when I was two and a half years old. Mum, Dad, Johnny, and I (along with Auntie, of course) moved to another rented house in Thames Ditton named "Kenray"—again, not far from the river.

Kenray was a little taller than Threesome. It has a decent-sized front garden with a large tree. I didn't like the atmosphere. In autumn, there seemed to be a swarm of spiders—pale brown with dark spots—weaving their webs amongst the withering irises and gladioli along the front path. As winter approached, I remembered the withered flowers, sodden and drooping in the rain, and the ice outlining the stalks.

One of these shows was where I made my first stage appearance. When I was three and a half, I performed "Wynken, Blynken, and Nod" with two other girls. Patricia ("Trish") Waters, for example, has remained a friend to this day. Trish's hat slipped over her eyes when we danced a polka onstage, and I reportedly continued to guide her around the platform so she wouldn't collapse. I guess I already knew the show had to go on!

Aunt once created "A Day at the Races," with herself playing the front legs and me playing the hind legs of the winning horse. We executed a weird dance, which I did blindly because my head was buried against Aunt's posterior. There was no air circulating in that enclosed space since the papier-mâché head was bonded together with strong-smelling glue. We fumbled through the dance, but when Auntie stepped out of the contraption, she passed out.

My mother and my father's mother had a falling out. Granny Elizabeth had clearly been a wonderful teacher and a fine mathematician, but she lacked tenderness and grace. She was bone thin, her face was lined, and her tongue could be keen. She once informed my mother that she would never have children since she was barren. There was no misunderstanding between them.

Betty, Dad's sad, demented sister, was present on one of my first visits to the house. I'm not sure what triggered it, but she had a nasty fit. My father, his mother, and someone else were arm-wrestling this wailing, drooling creature through the living room, up the stairs, and into her bedroom, closing the door behind her because she was so out of control. Her shouts, wrath, and inability to communicate her predicament terrified me, and I was immediately sent home.

Despite the fact that I only saw her once, the encounter stayed with me for many years.

World War II broke out in September of that year.

Hitler focused his forces on conquering Poland, followed by Norway and Denmark in the spring of 1940. This time period was dubbed

"The Phony War." Despite the fact that Germany and her European allies had declared war on one other, no side had mounted a substantial attack. This allowed England a very little window of opportunity to strengthen its fortifications. Because America had not yet entered the war, England attempted to prepare for the German advance on its own.

The national spirit was on display. Every able-bodied person was roused to assist, and the populace labored tirelessly. Uncle Bill joined the air force, but because of his technical skills, my father was deemed important to the domestic defense effort and was denied combat duty. Instead, he enlisted in the Home Guard.

One day, my father arrived home with gas masks for the entire family. After World War I, mustard gas was the greatest threat. Dad demonstrated what we needed to do and forced us to try them on.

Everything revolved around the battle. It was ever-present and ever-threatening. Hitler only needed to cross the English Channel...Our air force was smaller than the Luftwaffe's, but we had a good Royal Navy that kept our coast safe for the time being. However, German U-boats patrolled the waters, and they were so effective that convoys carrying essential supplies to Britain were frequently sunk. Rationing of food began in January 1940.

He worked all hours of the day and night. Sometimes he'd go home and sleep for an hour, or he'd nap at work on a tiny bench, then get up and keep going, because keeping going was so important.

He would occasionally take me down to Thames Ditton's riverside tavern. I couldn't go inside since I was underage, but he'd grab his drink and bring me a lemonade and some chips, and we'd sit there. I didn't understand why people liked to gather only to drink, but I could tell it was a pleasant break for my father.

My mother joined ENSA, or the Entertainments National Service Association, in early 1940, sarcastically dubbed "Every Night Something Awful." This was an organization formed during the war to provide amusement for British military service members. She traveled to France with Ted to entertain the troops. There were two children at home who needed her, but I believe the desire to accompany Ted was overwhelming.

One particular day before she went is indelible in my mind.

Mum took me on a walk, which was unusual because she rarely took walks with me. We walked hand in hand through the hamlet, through the shops—and I noticed a child's frock in a window. It was over-the-top, fluffy, and pink, yet it was the most beautiful thing I'd ever seen. A few days later, I returned home from an outing and noticed the house was vacant and that she had left. She hadn't even said goodbye. Though mom had been gone before, I had a feeling, as children do, that she was not going to return.

My first nightmare followed soon after. In my dream, an ugly goblin entered my bedroom through the open door and stood in front of me. I believed he was a buddy or a new toy at first, but then he pulled out a knife and I realized he was going to cut me.

I awoke in the dark, afraid of his presence. I needed to reach my father, so I made a frightened rush towards his room, certain that I would be attacked on the way.

Johnny was nestled next to my father in the huge bed, dozing. He recognized my sobbing dread and tucked me into warm sheets and the protection of his arms. Even yet, I couldn't express the dread that appeared to be ingrained in my soul.

Germany launched its "Blitzkrieg" invasion of France, Belgium, and Holland on May 10, 1940, the same day Winston Churchill was elected Prime Minister of the United Kingdom. Hitler pushed into France, meeting resistance along the way, and eventually made it to Paris. On June 23, he led his triumphant troops down the Champs Elysées, passing through the Arc de Triomphe. He had expected to find all of the riches of the Louvre Museum waiting for him, but they had all been removed, carried away, and concealed in chateaux and caverns around France in a short period of time. It's a miracle that Hitler never found them.

The German Army's might was such that British troops (and some French allies) were forced to retire to the English Channel beaches of Dunkirk, where they were repeatedly strafed by the Luftwaffe and many died. However, 340,000 soldiers were saved from the beaches by every civilian yacht, fishing vessel, barge, and motorized boat that could sail across the Channel from England, all of whom were summoned by Churchill.

My mother later told me that she and Ted had been entertaining troops in France when Hitler invaded, and that they had been lucky to get one of the final ferries to England before the borders closed; otherwise, they would have been incarcerated. I knew that if things had gone differently, I would not have had a mother at all, which made me appreciate her much more.

Hitler eventually switched his focus to Britain and began planning an invasion. He needed air superiority to be successful, thus he tasked his Luftwaffe with attacking the British air and coastal defenses first. The combat of Britain, which lasted from July to October 1940, was the first combat fought entirely in the air.
For me, the war came into sharp focus. Air raid sirens screamed frequently, particularly after midnight. The warden appeared.

As the bombing strikes became more frequent, we were often compelled to retreat into the Underground stations for safety, joining the crowds. I'd never taken the metro before. I recall descending long escalators to the station platform and inhaling that indelible smell of baked dust. Cots were arranged in stacks against the platform walls, as far away from the black pit and the scary electric rail—so alive that falling on it would kill you.

Another time, another air raid, my mother and Ted arrived late from somewhere to entertain. The warden arrived and knocked on every door in the apartment building, claiming that an incendiary device had been dropped nearby. The problem with incendiaries was that they would sometimes not ignite for hours after being dropped. This one was not found. Everyone was told to flee.

My mother and stepfather were so tired that they chose not to answer the phone. They were, I assume, the only ones remaining in the building, and they slid into bed softly. When my mother awoke and went into the kitchen to make a cup of tea, she gasped as she pulled back the blackout curtains, for there, snugly placed in the concrete square of the courtyard, was the incendiary bomb. They'd slept by it all night.

On November 14, nine hundred incendiary bombs were thrown on Coventry in ten hours, razing it to the ground. It was a devastating blow to the nation, and morale suffered greatly as a result.

Aunt Joan sent a brief telegram: "Married Bill yesterday in Gretna Green." "I adore Joan." Gretna Green is a picturesque Scottish location known for delivering quick weddings to eloping couples.

My mother was taken aback by the news. Joan, she thought (probably correctly), was upset with her for abandoning her and my father, and Joan simply married Bill to spite her. I got the idea that she was similarly upset about the marriage and thought it was foolish: that Bill was a kind guy, but quite frail. Caught up in the complexity and pressures of her new life, as well as what must have been a whirlwind of emotions, it was possible that it was the first time my mother considered the repercussions of her actions. Aunt's marriage closed another door, possibly one that Mum hadn't foreseen.

Aunt told me forty years later that my father had proposed to marry her for the sake of our children. After Mum departed, it was up to Dad and Auntie to take after Johnny and me, and despite the fact that it must have been difficult with Dad working and Aunt teaching, they did an excellent job. Aunt revealed that Dad had told her that he could never love her and that the marriage would be purely for practical reasons. Aunt had always secretly loved him, and years later she clung to him as a lifeline, which drove my father insane! Needless to say, they never married. Dad and Johnny relocated from Kenray to a little flat in Hinchley Wood, near Esher, Surrey, when Auntie married Bill.

Winifred Maud Hyde, a young widow, came to work at the Esher Filling Station plant. Pat Birkhead, her husband, was a bomb disposal specialist. Pat had just been married fourteen months when he was killed while defusing a bomb. Despite her loss, Win needed to find work. She was engaged as a captain lathe operator at Dad's company, working twelve-hour shifts. I once met her there, and I recall her wearing a snood to keep her hair clean and tidy and away from the machines. She was a lovely woman with lovely eyes who seemed genuine and nice. My father and Win became friends, and whenever time and the war effort allowed, they would travel to London for a day trip.

I remained in Walton with Uncle Bill Wilby's mother and stepfather, Aunt Paula (also known as "Auntie Caula") and Uncle Fred while Mum was there. Uncle Bill's parents were the only relatives I could stay with because Auntie Joan and Uncle Bill had moved to a flat in Belgravia. It was convenient because I could be close to my mum and visit her on occasion.

I stayed for two weeks while Mum was recovering after Donald's birth. (In those days, even if there were no complications, you had to stay in the hospital for that long after giving birth.) I was transported to the maternity hospital a couple of times, but because of my age, I was informed I couldn't go inside. Ted Andrews led me to the back of the house, where I sat in a rose bed and gazed out the window of her room. My mother smiled and waved as she held up the baby. I really missed her. I later discovered that Dad, unwilling to divorce, had promised to adopt Donald if Mum would return to him. It was another act of gallantry on his part, but it never happened.

Chapter 2

We relocated from Camden Town to Clarendon Street in Victoria not long after Donald was born. It was a little nicer ground-floor flat, with a sitting room and bedroom on the street level and a kitchen, bathroom, and living area beneath. Windows in the basement looked out upon a rectangle of concrete laid beneath a grid in the pavement, with three arched storage rooms with black painted doors on the other side. One of these served as our air raid shelter, another as storage, and the third as my bedroom. It had a whitewashed curved ceiling, similar to a crypt, and no windows. I recall lying in bed, afraid, listening to the crunch of bombs dropping during the night raids, and felt strangely safe being under the road. But I'm still afraid of explosions: fireworks, firearms, balloons—anything volatile and out of my control.

During the day, my mother would take baby Donald outside in his pram to get some fresh air. She would tie the pram to the railing outside our front door with a padlock and chain because we didn't have a garden. I was in the basement kitchen one morning, peering up through the grid, when I noticed a strange woman pick Donald out of his pram and go away with him.

Johnny and I were evacuated to Wrecclesham Farm in Farnham, Surrey, some thirty miles south of London, in September 1942. Aunt Joan joined us while Uncle Bill was abroad in the Royal Air Force, probably to watch after us because I was only six and Johnny was four. We should have gone to the west or north of England, where a lot of other kids were being taken.

Auntie Joan and I had a huge bedroom, while Johnny had a small closet down the way. Our room had a modest electric heater, and we slept with stone hot water bottles in the enormous bed. But the sheets were so wet that when touched by a warm body, steam practically erupted from them, and they smelled badly of mildew.

The property had a large amount of land. It was also a popular riding school, complete with stables and horses. The smell of the tack room, the leather saddles and bridles, and the overall sensory experience of the horses were all wonderful. Johnny and I would assist one of the local farm girls in lathering and cleaning the tack, as well as feeding and bringing the horses in from the fields at night. I noticed the smith working on the horses' hooves. Of course, I learnt to ride a horse.

The newscasters had serious names like Alvar Liddell and Bruce Belfrage, and they reported the news with precise accuracy and sharp diction in their solemn, well-cadenced accents. We would listen to Churchill speak, hanging on every word he said.

I had a good time at the farm. I'd returned to the countryside, and Johnny and I were together. But we didn't have a father or a mother. Every now and then, one of them would pay me a visit, and I would always beg, "Couldn't you stay?" But they couldn't because they were both so busy—Dad with the war effort, and Mum and Ted entertaining and keeping morale high. Thank goodness Auntie was present. She was a surrogate mother for much of my life, vibrant and exciting, and Johnny and I were fully reliant on her. "Oh, Auntie!" screamed little Johnny once. "Don't take me out without you!" became a family catchphrase.

There was a brief break in the conflict in the spring of 1943. I was reunited with my mother and Ted Andrews on Clarendon Street, while Johnny returned to Hinchley Wood to live with Daddy. At this point, two things occurred. Ted Andrews agreed to give me singing lessons while I was still in school. Aunt also left Wrecclesham, taking a one-room flat in London. She was teaching dance at the Cone-Ripman School, a performing arts school with academic programs in the morning and a variety of dance lessons in the afternoon. This was the school I went to. It appeared enormous at first, and I was only seven years old.

I'm not sure why Ted started teaching me to sing. My voice was "discovered" while singing to the family in the air raid shelters, but that was a publicity stunt concocted by my stepfather or the press. More likely, I was badly underfoot with nothing to do, and Dad decided to teach me lessons to keep me quiet. Or maybe it was an effort on his part to get to know this new stepdaughter who was afraid of him and didn't like him. In any case, it appears that he and my mother were taken aback when they discovered that my singing voice was extremely distinctive. It has a very wide range and strength for such a young age.

It was on Clarendon Street that I discovered my passion for reading. When I was very little, my father taught me to read, and it became my salvation. I could sit in a chair for hours and read. My mother, however, would call me out on it, saying, "That's quite enough for one day!" or "You're being lazy, wasting your time away!" Perhaps she had a valid reason; perhaps I needed to assist with the dishes, or maybe she was concerned about my strabismus or something, but I took it terribly, resenting her for denying me that delightful retreat. There was a point when I didn't read for quite some time. I felt bad about how much I adored it. Reading wasn't until later, when a tutor pushed me to study several classics, that I found myself enjoying reading again.

Mum and Ted decided to leave London during the war's monetary lull. They purchased a property on Cromwell Road in Beckenham, Kent, and we lived there for the following five years.

Kent is commonly referred to as "the garden of England" because of its orchards and fruit trees, and sections of it are stunning. However, it is the county in southeast England that borders the English Channel, and as such, it was directly on the flight line between Germany and London. As the Luftwaffe came home, any bombs that were not dropped on London were thrown on us.

My parents divorced just before we arrived, and my mother and Ted married immediately in a civil ceremony on November 25, 1943. Mum subsequently told me that she had planned to wait a bit before remarrying, but Ted Andrews was adamant—and then there was Donald.

I was given a puppy after we moved to Beckenham—an exquisite English cocker spaniel. With fragrant breath and pluggy feet, it was golden and wonderfully soft. Unfortunately, this adorable creature caught the condition that caused Saint Vitus' dance, and for some reason, my stepfather insisted on taking me to the vet to have the dog put down. I recall sitting in the car with it hopping and twitching in my lap as I tried to calm it down. I remained in the car while Pop took the small bundle inside. I was so depressed that I couldn't stand it.

I was touched by the gesture, but I wasn't sure what to do with the present. My mother gave me miniature cups and saucers to play "house" with, and I went out there every now and again, but it never completely worked. I didn't have any pals my own age, so no one came to play with me. I was alone in the garden, feeling a little damp and cold.

Everything was gloomy around that time, in retrospect. Mum seemed tense and out of sorts, and I could tell she was stressed. It's no surprise she was miserable, what with a new baby, dealing with the divorce, being newly married to Pop and mediating between us, organizing a new house, and her classical talents going mostly wasted.

The war escalated once more. Barrage balloons littered the London skyline, defending against low-flying aircraft. The night sky was littered with searchlights. Despite the danger, King George VI and Queen Elizabeth remained at Buckingham Palace to encourage the British people. Though they might have easily decided to hide away in the country, they never did, which is one of the reasons they are so cherished by the English. They went to bomb sites and hospitals, and they were a constant, soothing presence.

By the summer of 1944, the Germans began sending pilotless aircraft known as "doodlebugs" to England. We'd hear the pulsing drone of their approach, then a startling quiet as the engine cut out, followed by an unforgettable whistling sound as the missile hurtled into the ground. Because the doodlebugs had a penchant for swerving at the last second, if the aircraft cut out immediately overhead, one might be pretty certain of being safe. The threat was significant if they cut some distance out.

Because the raids were so frequent, we constantly ended up at the shelter. As the battle drew to a close, no housewife could do her laundry, bake a cake, or prepare a meal without interruption, for attacks came at all hours of the day and night. The sirens would blair incessantly, and the entire family would flee to safety until the all-clear signal was given. (I'm reminded of that all-clear sound every time I hear the local fire station's midday siren.)

We spent some nights in the air raid shelter. We'd talk quietly or listen for planes while huddling down there, feeling claustrophobic and wondering whether this was the day we'd be attacked. We'd hear the crunch of the bombs and count ourselves lucky that they only landed in a circle around us.

Dad and Win married on June 3, 1944. They spent their honeymoon in Brixham, on the south Devon coast, with Johnny in tow. Johnny had to sleep in their single room, which had a double bed. That first week, Win was on the verge of leaving the marriage since Johnny was a "little bugger" and nothing was going well. They made it through somehow. They utilized a tiny inheritance left to Win by her father to purchase a home in Chessington, Surrey.

I was going to return to Beckenham one day when I found myself standing in the tiny dining room, trying to gather myself. On the sideboard was a thick cut-glass bowl, and the sunlight was sending rainbow refractions off the glass. I reasoned that if I stared at the bowl long enough and hard enough, something about its sharp angles would make me stop crying. I stared and stared, hoping that the source of my pain would emanate from the crystal rather than my head and heart.

Autumn arrived, and classes at the Cone-Ripman School began in earnest, requiring me to travel to London every day. Aunt continued to teach dance at the school and live in her one-room apartment. Because I was only eight years old, it was arranged that I would live with her during the week and return to Beckenham on weekends.

Aunt and I were generally alone because Uncle Bill was away in the Air Force, billeted somewhere. I slept on a cot, while she slept in a single bed. When Uncle Bill arrived home on furlough, a screen was erected in front of my cot. They'd cuddle on the single bed, and Auntie would giddily shout out, "Julia, turn to the wall!"—a phrase that lingered with us for years.

Auntie and I had a rather hectic routine at Cone-Ripman School. In the mornings, there were academic sessions, and in the afternoons, there was ballet, tap, and character dancing. Miss Grace Cone, the principal ballet teacher, was a true martinet, constantly slamming her cane on the floor to accentuate musical beats. Miss Mackie, another teacher, was a stern and unpleasant woman. She gave tap courses and had no patience for anyone who was shy or unsure. She gave me the idea that I was completely hopeless. She appeared to have a thing against me for some reason. My feet could tap fairly well, but my arms were tight and uncoordinated. I frequently chose to hide towards the back of the class in the hopes that she would not pick on me...But she was relentless in her pursuit of me.

Mum decided that I was old enough in the spring, just after I turned nine, to attempt living in Beckenham full-time and taking the train to London and back on a regular basis. Aunt picked me up at Victoria Station in the mornings, drove me to school, and dropped me off at home in the afternoons. It was a half-hour journey each way, and I quickly felt fatigued. Not only did I have to get up early to fly to London and then work at school all day, but I still had schoolwork and vocal practice to do after returning in the evening.

Auntie unexpectedly appeared at our home not long after I moved back to Beckenham permanently. She held a telegram in her hand, announcing that Bill had been shot down over France. He had eluded arrest for 28 days before being apprehended and taken to a German prisoner-of-war camp, where he would spend the rest of the war. It was not one of the more known camps, and he was spared execution because he was an officer. But we were all worried about himar.

Pop continued to teach me to sing throughout this time. He tried everything he could to make friends, but I was having none of it. I was embarrassed, self-conscious, and intimidated by his physicality. He appeared to be a large and powerful man to me. He wasn't particularly tall, but he flexed his muscles, chewed loudly and juicily, and occasionally inhaled audibly through his nostrils. My father always appeared to be nice; Pop was odd, unusual, and explosive at times. To some extent, I was able to ignore the fact that I had a stepfather. I refused to admit that he and my mother shared a bedroom; it was always referred to as "my mother's room." I attempted to live side by side with him, as if he were a temporary guest in the house, and I truly despised the singing lessons. He merely worked on basic vocal exercises with me, but I was also expected to practice on my own for a half hour every day.

Soon after, though, I was sent to see Pop's vocal teacher. Lilian Stiles-Allen was her given name, however she was always addressed as "Madame." She had tutored Pop when he first moved to England from Canada, and she still offered him lessons on occasion. She was a small, stocky woman with thick ankles, a large rear, and a large bosom. She had a "pouter pigeon" look about her. Her belt was slung in a lovely V below her tummy, slightly to the left of center. She wore long skirts to her ankles and practical lace-up shoes on little feet that appeared too small to hold the frame above. She walked with a cane and typically wore a beautiful velvet coat and hat. Her attractive face had multiple jowls, but her eyes were stunning. Their long, spiky lashes caressed her cheeks, despite their small bulge. She would occasionally wear a trendy hat of the time, generally with a large sweeping brim or a feather. She was commanding, yet compassionate and kind, and she spoke in the sweetest, most mellifluous voice.

But my voice matured so quickly that by the age of nine and a half, it was clear that I was going to sing, and rather well. Pop returned to Madame and begged her to hire me, and she finally consented. My classes were no longer with Pop after that, which was a big relief for me. So my formal singing instruction began.

Initially, I took classes with Madame once a week. She lived in Leeds but commuted to London on a regular basis to teach at Weeke's Studios in Hanover Square.

Madame was a poor pianist with long, lovely fingernails that clacked away on the ivory keys. She always wore nice rings on her hands to keep her hands busy during the long hours of teaching. Her accompaniment was primarily "suggested," so you had to fill in the blanks in your head while singing, but it didn't matter because she was an excellent teacher.

She was a dramatic soprano well recognized for her performance as Old Nokomis in Samuel Coleridge-Taylor's Hiawatha at the Royal Albert Hall. She sang in many oratorios, concerts, and radio shows, and her singing voice had a flute-like tone, especially in her higher register. It seemed to pass down her nose rather than out of her throat. She had mastered a certain technique, and I later discovered that her voice resembled that of Kirsten Flagstad, the Norwegian soprano whom she adored.

We spent a lot of time practicing Handel, first with just the exercise vowels and later with the words: songs like "I Know That My Redeemer Liveth," "Rejoice" from the Messiah, and "Oh, Had I Jubal's Lyre." "When in doubt, return to Handel," Madame always remarked. Handel will never disappoint you vocally. Practice Handel whenever you can." She applauded the composer for his understanding of lyrics that vocalists may cling to in order to enhance their voices without harming them. Handel composed many extended passages that required good breath control, and these exercises were crucial.

Madame hoped that I would pursue a career in opera, but I always felt that it would be too much of a reach for me. My voice was incredibly high and thin, and while it was pure and clear, it lacked the guts and weight required for opera. Classical singers never need microphones because they fly above and above the orchestra. It's amazing to me how they do it. It's full-throttle singing, and while many operas only have around twenty minutes or so of pure, all-out vocal effort, it's still a question of lungs, volume, and strength.

Though Madame taught me the best technique possible, I believe her aim for me to go into opera and strive to duplicate her sound was ultimately impractical. I couldn't manage to discover what she called "that special place," despite my best efforts. My attempts frequently produced a constricted, nasal tone. Madame's technique was correct and safe—even failsafe for her—but it didn't allow for a certain reality in my opinion. I was "lifting" my voice into my head, which is necessary, but the nasal sound never seemed as natural to me as a slightly more open, released sound. When I eventually discovered my voice, it was a hybrid of everything she'd ever given me. After around fifteen years of working together, I knew enough to recognize what was correct and what wasn't, yet one never stops learning, thinking, feeling, and making voice choices that are as safe as possible. Maintenance and "refresher courses" are required.

However, there were other songs that I simply could not sing. Songs in a low note or with a wistful theme, such as "Songs My Mother Taught Me" or "O My Beloved Father," from Puccini's Gianni Schicchi. I was overcome by the lyric's anguish mixed with the sheer delicacy of a melody. As I choked, I could feel my throat shutting. I would fight tears for all I was worth, edging behind the piano bench so Mum couldn't see, but the voice would go in a flurry of emotion. Mum would turn around and see me sobbing uncontrollably.

I would cry for many reasons with Madame. When I couldn't get something right, I cried out of exhaustion, anger, or rage at myself. I suppose it was a catharsis to just let go because there was so much unrest in my breast.
Madame was always patient.

I took my Grade IV ballet exam just before the end of the academic year at Cone-Ripman and achieved a good grade. Then I worked for and took my Grade V, and something extraordinary occurred.

I recall standing in a school corridor, exhausted, awaiting my turn with the examiner. I could hear the pianist playing for the student ahead of me. I was scared, I felt unprepared, and I even wondered if I would be able to hold up due to my exhaustion. My body was rarely as strong as I required it to be. All of the other girls seemed upbeat and capable.

Nonetheless, I had become pale and chronically fatigued as a result of my singing classes, riding the train to school every day, dancing, doing schoolwork, and singing practice at night. My mother said as the summer vacation began, "You're not going back to Cone-Ripman," which was a huge comfort to me. I'd enrolled at Woodbrook, a local girls' school in Beckenham, and would start classes in the fall.

On May 8, 1945, Europe proclaimed peace. My mother, Pop, Don, and I headed to Walton-on-Thames to see friends and observe the festivities, and there was a wonderful sense of excitement everywhere: bonfires on village greens, people overflowing out of bars, flags waving in all directions. This became known as VE Day, which stands for Victory in Europe.

Almost immediately after, the press in Germany published the most heinous photos of concentration camps. The press was allowed in once our troops arrived and all of the camps were liberated. Our newspapers were plastered with headlines about the tragedies at Belsen, Auschwitz, and other concentration camps, and the photos were horrifying. The condition of the remaining detainees was beyond description, with some so malnourished that they couldn't move. I witnessed images of mass graves, with bodies piled one on top of the other and bones protruding everywhere. The images resembled Hieronymus Bosch's paintings, only worse, and England, like the rest of the world, was terrified.

Japan was still at war when the atomic bomb was detonated on Hiroshima, followed three days later by Nagasaki. VJ—Victory in Japan—was declared on August 14, 1945, and World War II was thankfully finished.

Mum and Pop's show always began with a theme tune. Pop's voice would be heard in the audience singing a refrain from the ballad "I Bring a Love Song." The curtains would part as he reached the final notes, and there they would be: my mother at the grand piano, the skirt of her dress draped prettily over her, and Pop in a dinner jacket at the microphone.

They began with classical arias, such as Pagliacci's tenor aria "Vesti la Giubba," or Rodolfo's first aria from La Bohème, "Che Gelida Manina." Pop performed them in English. They'd then sing a few ballads before Pop introduced Mum and she'd play a solo. Pop would eventually return with his guitar, and the two of them would finish the day's hit tunes. Their show had a certain level of sophistication to it; it was well thought out, and they performed for almost thirty minutes.

As planned, I started at Woodbrook in the fall. Miss Meade and Miss Evans, two aristocratic ladies who were undoubtedly partners in every sense, ran a good girls' school. It was my first formal academic experience, and I thoroughly enjoyed it. There was a period of stability after that, during which I made some companions my own age. I was in the school plays and really enjoyed them. I recall playing Robin Hood in a swashbuckling manner, with a lot of macho (or so I thought) thigh-slapping and posturing, legs akimbo, hands on hips, while I exclaimed, "Follow me, men!"

The students gathered in the main hall for roll call and hymn singing during morning congregation. This was a thrill because when the seniors sang the descants, my head was instantly filled with their magnificent counter-melodies. I rarely got the opportunity to sing choral work alongside others.

I was treated like any other student at Woodbrook. I was encouraged to participate in sports, which I was horrible at, and to join the Brownies. The issue was that I couldn't seem to locate my specialty. The Brownie pack would meet every week after school. There would be tests, such as knot tying (which I was quite good at), lighting a fire with only two sticks (which I was useless at), and other things at which I was absolutely terrible. I was hoping to make a name for myself in the fashion world, so I entered the competition for the best-dressed, neatest Brownie. I went to school, confident that I would pass with flying colors, but the Brownie pack leader saw a splotch of yellow egg yolk on my tie. Thank you very much!

On Saturday mornings, our local cinema showed children's programming such as cartoons, short films, and Westerns. The place was always crowded. I simply liked going whenever I could because it was a period of utter freedom for me when I lost myself in the wonder of Hollywood. I focused on the adventures of the Lone

Ranger, Roy Rogers, Gene Autry, Hopalong Cassidy, Mowgli, and Tarzan, oblivious to the chaos and clamor around me.

The Stage Door Canteen was a fantastic spot for the armed personnel to have a square meal, attend dances, and have some fun. They had been invited to play that evening, very likely because of my parents' relationship with ENSA, and had decided to bring me with them. I believe they thought it would enhance their act and make it an experience I would never forget. They were correct.

My parents sang a couple of songs before I sang an aria and a duet with Pop. Following that, Her Majesty appeared backstage in a magnificent beaded gown and brilliant tiara to greet the performers, who were arranged in a receiving line. She had a pleasantly attractive face and a charming and welcoming demeanor. She said to me when I curtsied, "You sang beautifully tonight," and then moved on to speak to my mother and stepfather.

Miss Meade, Miss Evans, and the kids were agog the next day at school. I was astounded at how impressed everyone was, especially the girls. It was my first taste of fame—the school klutz had become the center of attention. Everyone realized my parents were in "showbiz," and I appreciated finally being accepted.

Mum and I still wore our theatrical makeup on occasion. Pop hurriedly threw everything into the car in order to leave the theater and town and get a head start on the drive. We would stop at a transit café on one of England's lengthy roads around one-thirty in the morning. We'd pull into a run-down rest stop, its parking lot crammed with massive trucks and semis.

The cafés frequently had a large pot bellied burner inside, with a warm fug of smoke hanging in the air. It was a nice spot to be in the middle of a dreary night, with the fragrance of cooking and the fire burning. The truckers were pleasant, the place was crowded and vibrant with talk, and we would stop for bacon-and-egg sandwiches and scalding hot mugs of tea before continuing our journey.

We frequently traveled through rain and snow, and the sound of the windshield wipers swiping back and forth was quite comforting to me. The fogs were terrible back then—"pea soupers," as they were termed; fog thickened by coal smoke. My mother would take the wheel on such nights, and Pop would get out and stroll in front of the car with a flashlight. I'd wake up and lean over the front seat, staring ahead for any danger.

My mum had a lovely time in the north of England. She'd point out coal-mining communities and tell me about their history. She showed me the collieries with the massive wheels on towers, as well as shafts and lifts that went down into the mines below. There were slag piles, which were massive cone-shaped mountains of coal debris.

Sheffield was well-known for producing steel. I recall the mountainous streets and rows of identical houses with not a single tree in sight. It appeared dismal and plain black with soot to me. Every doorway, however, was whitewashed, and every window had white curtains. People in the North took great pride in keeping their pavements and doorsteps clean and their homes as spotless as possible.

I couldn't see anything redeemable about the North Country at the time; it simply appeared industrial and depressing. My mother, on the other hand, had childhood memories she wanted to share with me. I began to appreciate that region of England over time: the moors, the heather and gorse, the thin-steepled churches, the low stone walls, and little houses huddled into the hills and vales to shield themselves from the bitter winds.

In September 1945, Win gave birth to a baby girl called Celia, who became my half sister. I don't remember the day she was born, but I knew Win was having a child. I was initially upset that my father now had another little daughter in his life. Celia may have felt the same way about me as she grew older. We've now gotten quite close, but with a ten-year age difference between us, it was challenging at first.

Dad took Johnny, me, and Celia to Eastbourne one day. When we arrived at the beach, Dad went to change behind a rock. He then waded into the waves, followed by Johnny and Celia. I bravely waded in as well, not wanting to hurt or disappoint him. The wind was howling and it was very cold, but as I emerged from the water, my teeth chattering, I smiled and said, "Oh, Dad, this is the stuff of life!" I'm not sure why I said it—maybe because I knew it would delight him, perhaps because it was a healthy dose of truth, or perhaps there was triumph in having overcome the wind's chilling, piercing quality. Dad, on the other hand, never forgot. He frequently quoted me and took it to mean that I enjoyed those kinds of things, which I suppose I did. But I've always been a softie.

My mother gave birth to my youngest brother, Christopher Stuart Andrews, on May 12, 1946. Mum went back to Rodney House, Walton's maternity hospital.

This time, I stayed in the village with family friends Madge and Arthur Waters. Arthur was the manager of our neighborhood bank. Madge, his robust, hefty wife, was a member of the local Red Cross. They had two daughters, Virginia (Ginny) and Patricia (Trisha), the girl I danced with in Auntie's production of "Wynken, Blynken, and Nod," and who is still a good friend to this day.

Mum and Pop began returning to Walton-on-Thames on a regular basis to look for a new home. Mum's passion for Walton had never faded—it signified safety, roots, and everything she desired. Besides, their vaudeville performance was performing well, and they were probably ready to take a risk and make a name for themselves in the world.

They would always stop for lunch or tea with friends before going off to look at houses in the region on these trips. I was left to play with Trisha Waters at her house or Gladys and William Barker's residence.

Gladys was my mother's best friend. She had married William, who came from a long line of farmers and owned a magnificent market gardening business named Rivernook Farm. They were genuine and lovely individuals from the countryside. Uncle Bill was bombastic, larger-than-life but generous to a fault, and entirely reliant on his wife.

They had a son, John, and a daughter, Susan, who was a year younger than me. The Barkers adored children and had a dress-up box—a great trunk full of old clothing and trinkets, false jewelry, paper hats, and Christmas crowns—and, most of all, a summerhouse in their yard, a tiny structure with a very short porch extending out beneath the roof. It was ideal for a little theater.

"We've purchased a new house, and you're going to love it," Mum exclaimed one day. There are two acres of land and an owl in the garden." The prospect of an owl hooting in the middle of the night was unsettling, but Mum's enthusiasm for the location was evident. The house was to become what I now consider to be my childhood's true home.

Chapter 3

The house was known as "the old meuse" and was located at No. 1 West Grove, right on the border between Walton and Hersham. The street featured a row of run-down, Dickensian-looking almshouses on one side, but a long driveway to our house was about halfway up the other. The Belgrave Recovery Home, a convalescent community that was originally a beautiful mansion, was right next door to us. The Old Meuse had been the manor's servants' quarters, and my mother was overjoyed since her mother, Granny Julia, had served as a below-stairs maid there.

It was evident that this was Mum's dream home. It was considerably larger than anything we had ever occupied, and it was regarded as pretty upmarket at the time. I believe it cost exactly £11,000 (about $22,000 at today's currency rate), however home values have since skyrocketed to the millions. The cost was extremely exorbitant for my mother and stepfather. They had a large mortgage, and I quickly realized that they were overpaying for the property.

Except for mine, which was directly across from the bathroom, all of the bedrooms had sinks. There was one toilet upstairs, one downstairs with a washbasin, and one outdoors by the garage. The only source of heating was a little fireplace in almost every room.

Mum and Pop used emulsion paint to spruce up the entire property. They stuccoed the long, dark living room in white, then stippled a rose maroon color on top and added a high gloss finish. It was certainly stylish, but the walls appeared waxy, and with the warmth of a crowd or a fire, they would run with moisture.

I discovered a secret hiding spot down by the small copse beyond the tennis court—a little quirk of nature with the forsythia growing into a perfect natural arch. I'd lie on the ground and stare up at the yellow sprigs, daydreaming. I started to worry what I would do when I grew up. I didn't think I was excellent at anything, and I certainly didn't appreciate the significance of my voice at the time. I made a commitment to myself that whatever I did, I would do it to the best of my ability and contribute to society. If I were a secretary, I would be the best secretary in the world; if I were a florist, I would be the best florist in the world. I would work hard and apply myself to become valuable and needed.

Not long after they left, my aunt had the bright idea of turning the garages at the rear of the house into a dance studio. She and Uncle Bill moved into the bungalow, or "the bung," as we affectionately referred to it. Auntie named it "Twigs," and Uncle fashioned the name from garden branches and hung it above the door. The two-room prefab had no foundation and was only equipped with a Calor gas stove for cooking. In the large three-car garage, a mirror and ballet barre were constructed. Auntie's students used the outside toilet, which was renovated from a single garage. Auntie started her courses.

My mother used to play the piano for the dancing school, and the music would echo across the lawn, accompanied by Auntie's instructing, her hands clapping and maintaining time. I might see heads bobbing in the studio and hear Auntie's trilling giggle from our upstairs bathroom window, or hear her conversing with the mothers as she sorted coins for their payments. Though there was a lot of fun going on outdoors, the main home inside was typically silent, deserted, and dark.

I especially enjoyed watching the toddlers run and flutter around pretending to be fairies. Aunt was very patient with them, assisting in the strengthening and shaping of their little bodies and feet. If I wasn't studying or working, I'd go across to the studio and either participate in or observe the older children's courses. When Aunt could, she would give me special ballet lessons. She had some fantastic ballroom pupils who were eight to ten years my senior, and they eventually became known as "the gang." Keith Oldham, a gorgeous man with a glass eye, was one of his closest pals. He had a lovely girlfriend named Margaret, whom he later married. Ted Owen was a small guy called "Tappets" because he was always having problems with the tappets on his motorcycle.

I had seen the movie My Friend Flicka, about a lad and a lovely horse, at our local theater and had fallen madly in love with the star, Roddy McDowall. Ken McLaughlin, the man he played in the story, resided on the vast Goose Bar Ranch. I was so engrossed in the film that I dreamt about being married to Ken and having numerous properties and horses. After a day at the races with Uncle Bill, I would save the race card and laboriously copy all the horses' names, dams, sires, and pedigree facts into a ledger. My "Goose Bar Ranch" seemed extremely real to me, and I couldn't think of anything else for a time. I drew up property deeds, waxed them, and fastened them with scarlet string. They'd say something like, "This is to certify that Mr. and Mrs. Ken McLaughlin own the [name of ranch] and other parts of the United States and Canada." In the garden, I even kept a "stable" of Hadge's old beanpoles. I'd tie a string to one end and gallop the length of the land. In my mind, these were the cleanest, healthiest horses on the planet.

My mother appeared to be experiencing a new sense of well-being: she'd moved into her ideal house, had the two sons Pop desired, and their vaudeville show was doing well. Pop had joined one of the local golf clubs, where he spent a lot of time networking and socializing. He was a left-handed scratch player who was quite good—my mother referred to herself as a golfing widow. My stepfather's greatest ambition, I believe, was to win the British Amateur Golf Championship. Unfortunately, he never did.

That first year at The Meuse felt like we'd taken a giant leap forward in the world. So many wonderful things come to mind. Chris, the little trike rider, is working hard to learn to whistle. He couldn't say "Uncle Bill," so he called him "Dingle Bell"—a moniker we all took, ultimately shortening it to "Dingle" and later "Ding."

Our neighborhood movie theater occasionally screened Astaire-Rogers films. Aunt would make plans for us to see them whenever they were on. I believe she lived vicariously through celebrity marriage. We'd have so much fun—Aunt gushing over Ginger's beauty and clothes, and Fred's wonderful job throughout the film. I was likewise impressed, albeit more quietly, as I munched on my Mars bars. Aunt would take notes on every dance step she saw, practicing them by cavorting on the sidewalk all the way home, and incorporating them into her own choreographic works as soon as possible.

It appeared that things were finally going to be okay through pure hard effort and all of us pulling together. The divorce had been difficult, Mum's guilt had been overwhelming, and poverty had been crushing, but she and Pop were gradually constructing a better name and a better life for themselves. It was, in retrospect, the pinnacle of Mum and Pop's success and happiness. Unfortunately, everything went poorly from there.

I conducted my first BBC radio program just before relocating to The Old Meuse, at the Aeolian Hall on Bond Street in London. My parents were featured in the show. I'm not sure why I was invited to sing, but I sang "Polonaise" from Ambroise Thomas' opera Mignon. The engineers were telling me to move further from the microphone during practice because my voice was overpowering their sound system, but the broadcast went smoothly, which may have contributed to what happened afterwards.

The next thing I know, I was invited to take part in Mr. Parnell's new musical revue, Starlight Roof, in London. The London Hippodrome, located on the junction of Leicester Square and Charing Cross Road, was to host the production. I was given a one-year contract contingent on the success of the show.

Mum and Pop had been professionally represented by the agency of Lew and Leslie Grade (of television and film production fame, Lew eventually became Sir Lew, and finally Lord Grade). However, at this time, an American named Charles L. Tucker became their agent, and later mine. Charles was originally from Hartford, Connecticut. He was a huge, well-dressed man with a happy, moon-shaped face, gray, curly hair, and a great giggle. He used to be a vaudeville violinist in the United States, but he relocated to London and became a talent agent, representing some rather high-profile clients.

A small orchestra played in the pit, but there was also one onstage called George Melachrino's Starlight Orchestra. These were largely stringed instruments, and the musicians were excellent and dressed tastefully in white dinner jackets. Vic Oliver enjoyed directing; in fact, after the end of Starlight Roof, he traveled around England conducting several symphony orchestras.

The producers determined the day before our opening night that I appeared too naïve, too young to be in a sophisticated revue. My participation in the show seemed needless, if not inappropriate. I was going to be fired. Val Parnell and his aide Cissy Williams were attacked by Mum, Pop, and Charles Tucker. I recall standing back and waiting while they had a lengthy, intense discussion.

Mum and Pop requested that I sing "Polonaise" from Mignon, which I did. The "Polonaise" is a hundred times more difficult than "The Skater's Waltz"—it's a true coloratura tour de force, with a high F above top C at the end. The English translation is ridiculous beyond belief, but I blasted it out, leaping octaves and tearing off cadenzas and key changes with bravura and speed.

The premiere took place on October 23, 1947. Mum drove me to London on the train. We observed an English flower seller tucked into a convenient corner of Leicester Square, with her baskets and flowers spread about her, as we walked from the station to the theater.

When my big moment arrived later that evening, I ran fearlessly down the theatrical aisle. I got on onstage and performed "Polonaise" from Mignon, hitting that high F above top C at the end. There was a brief quiet before the audience erupted. People rose to their feet and continued to clap. My song literally brought the show to a halt. The aria was quite tough, and I was only twelve years old, a sprite of a thing with this strange voice, and it caused quite a stir. It was the first of three key career stepping stones for me.

That night, the reporters followed us home. They took pictures of me posing on the bed with my teddy bear and interrogated me. Needless to say, the flower vendor's present was a fortuitous one, and violets took on new significance for me in the years that followed.

We performed two shows every night except Sunday, with no matinées, for a total of twelve shows per week. It immediately became clear that I would be unable to attend school on a regular basis, therefore a tutor was engaged for me. The London County Council insisted on a chaperone to and from the theater, as well as a private dressing room, for minors under the age of fifteen. I was also not permitted to take a final curtain call with the group since the law prohibited me from appearing on stage after 10 p.m. Historically, children in the theater were treated horribly, so the government imposed stringent standards under the Child Labor Law.

My first tutor was a young, attractive, but ineffective woman whose name I can't recall. I walked all over her, telling her I was too busy to do her homework. Within two months, she was gone, and a new instructor, considerably older, Miss Gladys Knight, was hired—and she would accept no excuses. She was a strict disciplinarian, a sweetheart, and an excellent teacher. We worked together for four hours every day, and I finally started getting the education I deserved all along.

Auntie Mickey lived in Surbiton, three stops on the train line before Walton. We'd board the train together in London at the end of each evening, and she'd get off first at her stop, while I went on alone to mine. My folks would either pick me up or I would walk home.

Of course, there were evenings when my voice failed me. It wasn't frequently, but I occasionally swallowed or gargled my highest note out of pure exhaustion or worry. To be honest, I don't think any twelve-year-old should have been performing an aria twice a night for a year. I had the talent, but there were evenings in the smoke-filled theater (everyone smoked back then) when my vocal cords dried up and my famed high F didn't come out as beautifully as it should have. Other nights, it was as simple as it could be.

Because I was in the first half of the program and then had to wait through the second half plus the time between the shows, I had at least two hours between appearances. My chaperone and I would sometimes go out to Leicester Square for supper after I finished my homework, usually at a chain restaurant like Quality Inn or Forte's.

Leicester Square was flashy, smelled pungently, and shone brightly with neon, yet it was always a joy for me.

Uncle Bill—"Dingle"—was my favorite chaperone since he would frequently take me to the movies in between performances. In adjacent Charing Cross Road, there was a cinema that only played cartoons, and I had a great time seeing an hour of Mickey Mouse, Bugs Bunny, and other classic American animated comedies. After this delightful diversion, we'd return to the theater, where I'd sing my song again before being driven home.

During my time on the show, I had a huge crush on our main attraction, Vic Oliver. He was probably older than he appeared, with a balding spot in his hair, yet he seemed utterly suave, wearing an impeccable white evening jacket, and seemed the height of class and style to me. He was married to Winston Churchill's daughter, Sarah, and appeared to move in upper-class circles, always going to supper with a group of friends after the play. I started fantasizing about him and turned into a nasty groupie, lingering around the stage door hoping to say good night to him. I didn't know Pat Kirkwood well, but I did get to know her replacement, Jeannie Carson. Jeannie was a lovely and small member of the chorus. She took over for Pat multiple times and was well-liked throughout the firm. I later collaborated with her again, and she went on to make a reputation for herself in English musical theater.

There was also Michael Bentine. Michael was a young comedian with a shock of black hair and a huge toothy smile who was both handsome and intelligent. He appeared twice on the show, both times as a frantic, committed salesman. In the first section, he attempted to persuade the audience to buy a toilet plunger by demonstrating its multiple uses, such as a peg leg, a cap, or the electrical conduit connecting a tram to its cable. He returned later in the presentation with the upper half of a chair, touting the numerous functions of its lattice woodwork.

Michael met and wooed Clementina, a beautiful young ballerina in the chorus who was Marilyn Hightower's understudy, while performing in Starlight Roof. Later, Michael and Clementina married, and one of their sons, Richard, became my godson. Michael went on to have a tremendous career as a founding member of The Goons, brilliant performers who were the forerunners of the Monty Python crew, alongside Spike Milligan, Harry Secombe, and Peter Sellers. Michael was out of the ordinary, lively, and eager. One couldn't help but fall in love with him, and he became a longtime friend.

I was also invited to do a screen test for Joe Pasternak, a major film producer from the United States who had produced all of Deanna Durbin's films. Deanna was a well-known young soprano in Hollywood, and I was frequently compared to her.

The screen test was held at MGM Studios in Elstree, London. A number of still photos were taken, but it quickly became clear that they wanted to gussy me up a bit because I was so plain. My hair was curled into ringlets by the hair department, and I ended up looking like a grotesque version of Shirley Temple. We kept going.

Following the screen test debacle, my mother decided I should take acting lessons, and for a time, a local theater teacher came over to The Meuse to tutor me. I recall working on Shakespeare's Romeo and Juliet's death scene.

I must have done well enough to be entered for an early grade exam. I was sure I'd fail because I couldn't read music, but I performed my Clementi pieces with gusto, and the examiner looked impressed. To my complete amazement, I received the highest grade for that exam in the entire county of Surrey. I was astounded—somehow, I got a "highly commended," and the county gave me a book on Schubert's life as a prize.

Aunt Joan became pregnant during the run of Starlight Roof. She had always had a great thin figure as a dancer. She stayed slender, dressed nicely, and looked gorgeous throughout her pregnancy. I got the impression she wasn't delighted about being pregnant, but she could just have been anxious. Throughout her term, she continued to teach.

On April 21, 1948, Geoffrey Wilby was born. It was a violent and difficult delivery, and the tiny boy's head was severely injured by forceps. He passed away eight days later. For a while, our house was very quiet. Auntie returned home in tears. My mother looked after her, while my brothers and I kept our distance. Aunt's health began to deteriorate, which did not bode well for her marriage to Uncle Bill. I don't think Auntie ever tried to get pregnant again, and I know she still regretted the death of her son many years afterwards. My mother made a cruel remark to me at one point, which reflected the two sisters' love-hate relationship.

I was only able to play in Starlight Roof for one year due to County Council regulations, and that year sped by. I couldn't sing on the day of my final performance because I was so overcome with melancholy. As I made my way back through the audience and around backstage, the group applauded and roared.

My mother had forbidden me from opening any of my fan mail. The stage doorman would give me a packet of whatever letters came for me while I was in the performance, and I would take them home to her. Mum was concerned that disturbed individuals would write to me and say inappropriate things. She also refused to let me discuss my pay, claiming that "one does not talk about how much money one earns, nor does one ever ask other people." I was merely told that money was being deposited into an account for me, though I'm sure it was also used to assist with family needs. I was given a weekly stipend of two shillings and sixpence, which was increased to one pound once I started working consistently.

It was an invitation—no, a command—to perform in the Royal Variety Performance that year. It had been in my pocket for two weeks, and the deadline for responding was the following day.

This "Royal Command Performance" (as it is properly titled) is an annual one-night show that attracts the top talent in the country and earns enormous sums for charity. The Royal Family is always present, and it is always a spectacular and glorious evening for everyone involved, including the Royals. Danny Kaye was supposed to headline because he was performing at the London Palladium that year. I was supposed to sing the "Polonaise" with Melachrinos Starlight Orchestra, but to my surprise, I was asked to lead the entire company in "God Save the King " at the end.

I have a photograph of that night taken from the side of the theater that I love. I'm on stage, and the Queen, Princess Elizabeth, and Prince Philip are watching with the rest of the audience. I was tenth on the program, according to a placard to the right of the proscenium. It was given to me by a press photographer, and I kept it for years, forgotten and crumpled. When I discovered it again, I realized how important it was and had it restored. It is presently on display in my office.

My mother thought my thirteenth birthday was an excellent reason to throw a party. She was good at making basic gowns for me on her sewing machine, usually out of strips of gathered material hemmed in tiers for the skirt. They were usually attractive and inexpensive to produce. She sewed me an evening gown out of pink cotton that was shirred at the bodice for this party. The night before the party, she finished it.
We had just gotten a new dog, a corgi. His pedigree name was "Whisper of Whey," but Auntie, who had a knack for naming everything, said "Let's call him 'Hush.'" Unfortunately, Hush was often taunted by my brothers, who were too little to know any better, and as a result he became manic and snapped at everyone.

I knew I was still innocent, unrestricted in any manner. I was still young enough that my parents were in charge of my profession; I had no taxes to pay and no major responsibilities. I could notice my mother's and stepfather's troubles since I wasn't yet burdened by the responsibilities of adulthood. I knew that boys and all the craziness of adulthood would soon attack me, and I realized that this was probably the last time in my life that I would be relatively unpressured.

My parents received an invitation to play the egg in a pantomime of Humpty Dumpty at a theater called the London Casino a few weeks after I ended playing in Starlight Roof. Another job! What a miracle!

English pantomimes are seasonal Christmas extravaganzas mostly for children, though adults join in on the enjoyment. They are almost invariably based on classic fairy tales such as "Cinderella," "Red Riding Hood," "Aladdin," "Jack and the Beanstalk," "Mother Goose," and "Dick Whittington." If a narrative is produced in London one year, it is likely to be distributed throughout the provinces the next year, but with smaller sets to accommodate the new venue.

Emile Littler wrote, produced, and directed Humpty Dumpty. Emile and Prince Littler were impresario brothers who rose to prominence in the West End and the provinces, holding a virtual monopoly on the production of musicals and pantomimes across the country. Prince was significantly more well-known, having taken over as chairman of Moss Empires in 1947, which included the largest theater circuit in England. It was rated an "A" tour if one booked a Moss Empires tour.

Pantomimes are not mimed shows, as the name suggests. Not at all. Pantomimes did not have individual songs composed for them like they do now, albeit they were musical in content. Because popular music of the day was integrated into the old legends, the scripts frequently sounded absurd. "Oh, dear Princess, I love you so much that...," the Prince would remark to her.(keyboard key note)...I'd want to take you to Chi-na on a slow boat..."

Humpty Dumpty was an outlier in comparison to the relative elegance of Starlight Roof (and even other pantomimes). Tiddley-Winks, Penelope the Horse, and...the Wuffem-proof were among the cast members. The latter was a lengthy piece of blue feathery material. Pantomimes encourage audience engagement, and in this case, spectators were instructed to shout a warning if they saw the Waffen-proof. The Wuffem-proof would appear in any scene, moving around the set or appearing on the wall behind someone's head over the proscenium. The audience, particularly the youngsters, would go insane, shrieking, "Look out, it's behind you!" (To this day, most pantos incorporate similar activities, and "It's behind you!" is a stock phrase associated with the genre.)

I spent a significant amount of time driving back and forth to the theater. I don't recall seeing a regular chaperone, though there must have been one. I recall sitting on the train by myself, with orange pancake makeup all over my legs. They were generally pale and slender, with the ability to bowl a hoop through them. At the time, my self-description was "boss-eyed, buck-toothed, and bandy." It was suggested that I paint my legs to give the show a more youthful appearance. I'd apply the color in the evening and be so weary by the time I arrived home that I didn't bother washing it off. If we had a matinée the next day, which we frequently had, it didn't seem worth having a bath to remove it because it would be on again so soon—so I'd get back on the train with the makeup still on my legs, really streaky now! I'm not sure how bad my sheets were back then, but I recall receiving some strange looks on the train.

My mother encouraged me to go for walks with Tony now that he was a buddy and a respectable lad. Tony would arrive on the drive just as my lessons with Miss Knight were wrapping up for the day, pushing or riding his bike, and I would either ride my own bike or walk with him. The road up to the station, then over and down toward the Half-Way House (a local tavern on our village green), then back up West Grove. These walks provided Tony and myself with numerous opportunities to converse.

We talked for hours about what we both enjoyed, how he felt at school, and what he did there. He was extremely creative, developing school theater projects and building and manipulating puppets for a production of The Magic Flute that he also directed. I told him I liked to write stories in my spare time and came up with themes for two stories about orchestras: "Conceited Mister Concerto" and "Peter Piccolo's Great Idea." Tony offered to draw them. While he was at boarding school, letters and drawings from "Peter Piccolo" or "Mister Concerto" arrived in the mail on a regular basis.

One day, Tony's parents asked if I wanted to accompany them to Tony's college for the summer picnic, a yearly event known as "Gaudy." I went with some apprehension. I wasn't sure how I should act or if I would appear proper.

The Waltons impressed my mother. I believe she envied Dawn. Dawn was fortunate, she claimed, to be placed on such a magnificent pedestal by her husband. Mum didn't hold anything against Dawn, but she yearned for her way of life. We must have felt on a lesser social level than this gorgeous family.

Dr. and Mrs. Walton enjoyed business visits to America on occasion, where Dawn could also get some sun for her arthritis. When they realized that young Carol was upset that they were leaving, they just packed her up and carried her with them.

Every summer, the entire family spent a great vacation at a hotel on the South Coast, just outside Bournemouth. When they were gone and I didn't see Tony, I had an empty feeling.

Their house was beautifully adorned for Christmas, and mistletoe was hanging over the front door. Tony had hoped to kiss me there, but I was too bashful and refused to participate. I guess he won with a kiss on the cheek.

Many people were surprised when Winston Churchill, who had done so much to lead the country throughout World War II, was not re-elected after the war. Clement Attlee became Prime Minister after the Labor Party secured power.

Polio has been spreading steadily across America and England. Dr. Walton was a big fan of Sister Kenny, a nurse who was a pioneer in the treatment of infantile paralysis, cerebral palsy, and polio in the United States. In England, he grew passionate about adopting her methods, reinvigorating tissue using fascia massage and heat, which helped restore circulation to seemingly dead places. I assisted in the christening and opening of Dr. Walton's home for polio sufferers, known as "Silverwood." He was truly a man ahead of his time.

Chapter 4

Mun, Pop, and I worked in Blackpool, the most popular resort on England's northwest coast, during the summer of 1949.

Blackpool was a neon riot, but everything seemed dark and frightening to me. The stink of fish and chips, ale, and toilets along the seashore, the seething mass of humanity that moved from pier to pier, and the trams that rattled by continually formed a very sinister backdrop for the events that followed.

I was working at the Hippodrome in the heart of Blackpool in a variety show called Coconut Grove, which was similar to Starlight Roof. Jewel and Warriss, a comedy combo, headed the bill, along with Jeannie Carson (Pat Kirkwood's understudy from Starlight Roof, who had since come into her own) and Wally Boag. My stage name was "Julie Andrews—Melody of Youth." I came out of the audience once more to receive a balloon toy from Wally, and I sang an aria twice a night.

I didn't get to witness much of my own act since a taxi would take me to the Central Pier, where my parents were performing. I'd either walk the pier with Donald and play the slot machines like the tourists, or I'd watch Mum and Pop's program. The taxi would then return me to the Hippodrome in time for my second appearance, and then take me home.

He and my mother started arguing. When they returned home, there would be shouted shouts, scuffles, and thumps, followed by my stepfather slamming out of their bedroom and into the guest room.

I laid in bed, listening, afraid of what might happen—what Pop would do to my mother. She seemed to frequently bait him. She was undoubtedly upset about his inebriation onstage, but I sensed something deeper as well. Perhaps she felt compelled to mimic her father's beating because she had one. It appeared to me that whipping him up to the point of becoming aggressive was practically a delight for her. I had the feeling she'd physically press herself against him, and he'd fling her off, and she'd scream, "No, Ted, NO!" It appeared to be almost ritualistic in nature.

I would occasionally come out of my room to attempt to stop them—my room was next door to theirs on the same floor—and it worked occasionally, but most of the time I was too scared. I slept with only a vest and underpants and didn't have a dressing gown, so I felt underdressed, chilled with anxiety, and humiliated to reveal myself to Pop. Don and Chris were sleeping on the floor above us. Donald once came downstairs due to the noise, but I grabbed him up and brought him away.

There was a tremendous argument one night, and I heard my mother crying. There was a huge scuffle, then a loud thud, and I knew she'd fallen. My stepfather slammed into the guest bedroom, and I had no choice but to go check on her.

Auntie arrived as soon as she could. I'm not sure if she came more for us kids or for my mother, but having someone else in the house gave me a sense of security. It lifted a weight off my shoulders—I didn't feel as responsible for the boys, the house, or my mother's well-being.

Auntie remained for the remainder of the summer. Pop made an effort to gather himself, and with Aunt in the home, he seemed to settle down for a while. I'm sure he was annoyed that she came, because she was always a thorn in his side. In any event, the improvement was fleeting.

During this time, a press photo was taken of the family walking along the front of Blackpool, looking extremely cheerful. My brothers and I still wonder at how far that snapshot was from the reality of what was going on.

Depending on my schedule, Mum would occasionally send me away for a weekend to visit Dad. Chris was three years old, and I had been caring for him since he was a newborn, changing his diapers and tending to him. Even then, I didn't believe he was receiving adequate care. But now I was looking after Donald as well, making them both lunch and ironing. My mother seemed to be disappearing more and more, and I was constantly afraid of leaving them.

Pop became more abusive as he drank more. Donald received his first caning when he was just six years old. Pop stepped in and had a walking stick at him since he had a less-than-perfect report card from school. After that, Donald seemed to be in trouble all the time, and he was caned three or four times a year. My mother got despondent as a result of his misdeeds, and Pop would lead him away to the frigid front living room with the horrible pink stucco.

I'd stand in the dark corridor, listening to the thwack of the stick or strap and the muffled sobs from the other side of the door. I'd be terrified, astounded by the severity of the sin being visited on a young, helpless soul, and wondering how he could stand it.

I did nothing to halt the beatings, which went on for so long that I felt Pop was enjoying it or couldn't stop himself. When the door was opened, Donald would emerge with red, bloated, tear-stained cheeks, visibly ashamed that his family was aware of his plight, his spirit battered into submission. Still, I did nothing out of fear of taking sides, of becoming the next victim if I sought out. My mind would flip on a dime and I'd think, "Well, he had been naughty."

Donald would act normally for a while, until his fury rose up again and it happened all over again. His relationship with Pop became increasingly tense. He would follow his father to the golf range to recover golf balls, and he claimed Pop would aim them in his direction, requiring the youngster to dodge them while retrieving them. He finally hurled all the golf balls over the garden wall into the Belgrave Recovery Home greenhouse, resulting in yet another caning.

Donald subsequently informed me that when he was sixteen, right before leaving The Meuse for two years in the Merchant Navy, he went into Pop's bedroom, pulled out the canes that were kept in an overhead closet, and meticulously smashed every single one in front of his father. Congratulations to him!

Chris began boarding school a year or two later, when he was just four years old. He was quite homesick, and he was bedwetting a lot. It was devastating. I'm not sure who suggested the boarding school or how Mum felt about sending Don and Chris away—whether she felt guilty or not. Perhaps she thought the boys would be safer. I promised never to do so to my own children and feared being sent away as well.

Dad and Win relocated to Ockley, a settlement on the Sussex/Surrey border. Dad claimed that Ockley had the ideal educational distribution: one school, two churches, and four pubs.

He and Win purchased a semi-detached cottage in a series of five that had previously served as the gardeners' quarters for a large estate. Despite its modest appearance, "Leith Vale" enjoyed a magnificent outlook across the fields to the manor home.

One of our favorite parts was driving up Leith Hill, which overlooks Ockley. Tiny hamlets cling to the hillside, while trees on the crown form enormous arches over the narrow paths. The South Downs can be seen from the top, and my father would point out Chanctonbury Ring, a perfect circle of trees on another hill in the distance that was likely a Druid site. Dad showed me vestiges of an old Roman road that once ran through the countryside but is now mostly covered. An eccentric had built a tower on top of Leith Hill in order to raise the elevation to exactly 1000 feet. In the late spring, Leith Hill becomes a sea of bluebells, a shimmering haze in every direction.

Farmland surrounding Leith Vale. Johnny made me sick with laughter when he roared from his bedroom window like a cow and received an answering call from the bull at Standon Farm, across the lane. He and I went out for a late-afternoon walk when we noticed a big bird with a bullet head and an enormous wingspan coming extremely low along the path toward us. It was the barn owl from the neighborhood. It didn't notice us until we were fairly close, at which point it darted into a neighboring tree. Johnny and I waited motionless, waiting to see what the owl would do next. It descended from the tree in a straight dive after tilting its head from side to side many times. It lifted off, a tiny mouse in its beak, and flew right by us again, its big wings beating on the grass. We hurried home to tell Dad about our exciting adventure.

Dad's first priority, wherever he lived, was his garden, and I recall him sweating it out at Ockley, growing stands of runner beans and rows of potatoes, which were crucial to the family. Dad would take a wheelbarrow out to the neighboring ditches and dig up large, hefty clusters of leaf mold. He worked it into the garden soil, supplying it with all the nutrients it required.

Win would prepare delicious dinners with fresh beans, potatoes, tomatoes, and peas from their small allotment. My relationship with her was tense at the time. When I visited, I suppose it was a chore for her, but like any good stepparent, she understood and accepted my minor antagonism. She understood how vital it was for me to spend time with my father.

After that tragic summer in Blackpool, Mun and I didn't do any touring with Pop. From "Ted and Barbara Andrews—with Julie (in small letters underneath)," their billing was now changed to "Julie Andrews—with Ted and Barbara." It had to irritate my stepfather and make him feel emasculated. Despite the fact that he was the one who inspired me to sing in the first place, I believe being displaced by a fourteen-year-old stepdaughter pained him.

Mum and Pop had supposedly spent every cash they had on The Meuse, and they were now far over their heads. My mother's chats about it were fairly open, and there was a continual worry in the back of my mind that unless I kept working, we would lose our home. In reality, we most likely would have. It was critical to me that we keep it—the prospect of returning to a location like Mornington Crescent was intolerable. When gigs came along and Pop wasn't asked, Mum and I took what we could. I continued my studies with Miss Knight in the interim.

The more Mum and I performed alone, the better my performance became. I'd sing a few arias, then a ballad, then she'd play a piano solo, and then I'd come back and do a large medley, followed by a farewell song, with my mother accompanying me. It was structured similarly to the show she and Pop had been performing for years.

There are also humorous memories, notably of the personalities we encountered and the acts who performed on the same bill as us. Albert Modley, a comedian from the North Country, was one of them. He never played in the south of England, but he was a big hit up north. He was a really cheeky and adorable young fellow. He pretended to be a mischievous schoolboy, and part of his act included playing with a set of drums. He simply played with them on occasion, slamming the bass drum or banging a cymbal. He'd pretend to be a tram driver, whirling the cymbal arm and the cymbal itself round and round, as if it were the lever that drove the tram.

We were once on the same bill as Albert, along with a bear act. When the bears were performing, no one was allowed to cross behind the backdrop because the bears invariably turned and attacked whomever they thought was behind them.

My mother went to the bar for her usual drink one night after making me promise to stay safe in our dressing room. She shut the door behind her because the bears had passed through our corridor on their way to the stage. I was surprised to hear the doorknob rattling and whimpering from the other side. I was stiff with panic until I realized it was only Albert tormenting me and having a great time.

Mum frequently returned from these outings to the bar rather tipsy, and as a result, the second performance was never as good as the first. She would dominate the accompaniment, slamming the piano and urging me on if I tried to make a lovely rallentando or express myself in any manner. I'd graciously introduce her solo, and she'd perform something like "The Dream of Olwen"—a really corny song with her renowned double octaves added at the end, all of which she now fluffed horribly.

I kept working with Madame Stiles-Allen. Early in our relationship, she chose to leave London and return to Yorkshire, where she was raised. Once she relocated permanently north, it became clear that the only way for my voice to continue to grow and for me to take my lessons seriously was to travel up there to learn with her. Sometimes it would be for a long weekend, other times for a full week.

She lived in a sprawling, half-timbered farmhouse in Headingley, a village just outside Leeds. "The Old Farm" contained a massive kitchen that also served as a dining area, as well as an Aga cooker and a large fireplace. The furniture was vintage but cozy, with loose floral-patterned slipcovers on the sofas and chairs. In the main corridor, there was a genuine spinning wheel, and its spools and treadle, conjuring another age, piqued my interest. Gas bulbs flashing above the tiny gas jets illuminated the halls.

Her enormous, grand piano, and an antique, hand-cranked phonograph on which we would listen to 78-rpm records of Caruso, Gigli, Galli-Curci, and Adelina Patti were all housed in a vast, upstairs music room. The room was rarely used, owing mostly to the high cost of heating in the severely cold, damp winters. Madame mostly worked with her students in the smaller teaching room adjacent to it, which included an upright piano and an electric fire.

I would occasionally sit in on other students' classes. Madame thought this was vital, and I learned a lot just by observing and listening. Simply talking with Madame revealed to me that my voice had a higher tone. Madame's voice was so sweet and melodious—and so beautifully placed—that I found myself raising in imitation.

When the fire's embers died out, Madame and Jeff went to their bedroom at one end of the house, and I went to mine, down a long, drafty, gas-lit corridor to a very chilly room with a chamber pot under the bed. I never dared to leave the covers, not only because of the freezing temperature, but also because I was convinced the location was haunted. I'd burrow down and hide, practically drowning myself. I didn't get much sleep.

During my adolescence, I frequented Leeds. My mother would instantly ask me to sing for her so she could hear if I had improved when I returned home with my voice crisper and stronger.

Madame would still come down to London on occasion, and I'd be able to pick up a quick lesson with her. She used to stay with us in Walton. She and my mother had lengthy conversations about spiritualism, particularly reincarnation. Madame completely believed in it, and she was convinced that I was the reincarnation of the legendary soprano Adelina Patti. My superstitious mother enjoyed the excitement of believing in reincarnation. I was terrified by their uncanny chats and eventually chose not to listen to them, because my nights after that became filled with the dread that ghosts were coming out of my closet or that someone who had "passed on" could want to contact me.

Madame came to a radio show I was doing while she was visiting us. I sang the aria from La Traviata, beginning with the recitative "Ah, fors'è lui," and ending with the demanding "Sempre Libera." Before the main aria begins, there is an à cappella cadenza. My pitch was typically perfect, but because Madame was in the audience, I pushed too hard to sing right for her, and I started listening to myself. As a result, when I ended the cadenza, I landed a halftone higher. As the orchestra began to play the tune, I realized I was off key. My mother, who was present in the audience, chastised me for my error. I'm sure she wanted me to shine as much as I did for Madame. I was ashamed that I had messed up, especially since this was a live radio broadcast. I was just as harsh on myself as everybody else.

According to my auntie, my father was so in love with my mother that he decided it didn't matter. Johnny, his legal son, was born two years later. My mother had an affair with Pop several years later and became pregnant with Donald. The fact that Dad offered to take me, and later Donald, under his wing in order to keep the marriage together is remarkable. He never treated me differently whether he was aware of my origins. I believe he cared deeply about me. And because I didn't know he knew at the time, I didn't have the courage to confront him about it before he died. I thought I was shielding him from terrible pain.

I also never asked my stepmother, Win. And I never told any of my siblings about it. I really wasn't sure of my facts until I spoke with Auntie, so I didn't want to upset the apple cart. When I started writing this book, I thought they needed to hear the truth from me before they published my narrative. I wasn't thrilled to be the carrier of such bad news, but it felt necessary to set the record straight. It was a difficult time for all of us.

The essential point is that my feelings for the man I considered to be my father, Ted Wells, remained unchanged. I was adamant about it, and after that, I didn't want anything to do with the other man. I wasn't interested; I didn't want to start a relationship. I despised him as the specter that he was. I didn't see him again for another nine years.

Things The relationship between Mum and Pop deteriorated significantly. My mother appeared to be sinking deeper into depression, finances were becoming increasingly tough, and we were having difficulty making house payments. The Meuse was becoming overgrown. There was a mouse in my bedroom, and it ran over my hair at one point, which terrified me. I started hearing voices in my head at night, a frantic chatter, and I was afraid I'd go insane like Betty, my father's sister.

The late-night train that rattled through the local railway station was a source of comfort for me. I'd hear the steam engine's wheels clattering over the railroad ties, puffs of the chimney, and whistle shrieks as it approached from the coast to London. The sounds were usually calming when I was lying in the dark. They hinted that there was life out there...that the world was going about its business, which made me feel a little better.

I was looking out my bedroom window one day not long after my mother's disclosure, feeling a little sorry for myself. I stood in the garden, staring at the birds as they swooped down and around the rosebushes.

Uncle Hadge had long since left for London with Auntie Kit, and the harsh reality was that all the magic he had created in that garden had crumbled. things were critical to me that things not fall back into disarray, yet it had. The tennis court had become overgrown, the roses had gone wild, the gladioli had become spindly, and everything was in general disarray. It seemed to represent our family's situation.

It was a hot summer afternoon that was still and beautiful. It started to rain lightly at first, but gradually turned into fat, heavy drips. "Someone sent me a sign that there is something better in the world, something beautiful and worthwhile, something more to life than this," I reasoned.

I was admiring a particularly large, full-blown rose when one more raindrop proved too much for it. Its petals all fell to the earth at once. It was both surprising and strangely comfortable.

In June 1950, I began working as a resident performer on Educating Archie, a weekly BBC radio show. The show was originally slated for a six-week run as filler for popular ventriloquist Peter Brough and his dummy, "Archie Andrews," but ended up running for thirty consecutive weeks without a break and playing to a regular audience of about twelve million listeners.

I was said to be the little girl next door. I got a couple lines with the dummy if I was lucky; if not, I just sang. Working closely with Mum and Madame, I learnt many new songs and arias, such as "The Shadow Song" from Dinorah; "The Wren"; waltz tunes from Romeo and Juliet and Tom Jones; "Invitation to the Dance"; "The Blue Danube"; "Caro Nome" from Rigoletto; and "Lo, Hear the Gentle Lark."

Though it was not televised live, the program was recorded in front of a live audience, and I was able to observe several of the read-throughs as well as the show itself. I'd practice my one aria, then listen to these wonderful comedians and actors perform for radio. Many excellent artists featured on the show, including Tony Hancock, Harry Secombe, and Alfred Marks, all of whom went on to become major headliners. Many of the screenplays were written by Eric Sykes, who eventually became a well-known comedian.

On June 6, 1950, the first episode of Educating Archie aired. I was able to continue traveling with Mum sometimes because we only taped one day a week and I wasn't in every episode.

Mr. Fielding was a small, impeccably dressed gentleman who was usually cheerful and kind. He seemed to care about me, and I enjoyed working for him. His concerts felt like a step up in the world to me, and I was on the bill with wonderful performers: The Western Brothers, who did satirical monologues to music; Elsie and Doris Waters, who chatted about insignificant things; Rawicz and Landauer, a piano duo; Anne Ziegler and Webster Booth, the British stage's Jeanette MacDonald and Nelson Eddy; Larry Adler, harmonica player, and Joyce Grenfell, a gentle come

Mum and I were booked to perform in Eastbourne on a particular Bank Holiday. I had told my mother that I was old enough to pack my own theatrical equipment, and I did just that. We traveled to the south coast amid torrential rain. It appeared to be the wettest Bank Holiday ever.

The Winter Garden lacked footlights, so the audience couldn't be sure they were seeing what they believed they were seeing. Throughout my performance, heads craned and a buzz of murmured comments persisted. I tried hiding one foot behind the other and then reversing them, but it didn't work. Mum hammered away at the piano with vigor, I performed my songs quicker than usual—and I was never happier to leave the stage. I felt ashamed; there would be no additional bows for me that night.

I turned fifteen on October 1 and was formally released from the London County Council's child performer restrictions. My mother decided that Miss Knight, my tutor, was no longer required, and thus my formal education came to an end.

Mum planned one of her fantastic parties to mark my "liberation." The mansion must have held around sixty people. Everyone danced, jitterbugged, and had a great time. Don and Chris, who had been sent to bed, slipped out through the banister railings to see the celebration.

We stopped for a snack at some time, and Pop made a really improper remark about me and my pals, Susan Barker and Patricia Waters. I don't remember what he said, but Gladdy Barker was becoming increasingly agitated by his intoxicated conduct. She quickly scooped up a large plate of blancmange—a milky, jelly-like English pudding—on the table adjacent and tossed it at him. Pop ducked just in time, and it smacked into the wall behind him. Everyone in the room was silent as they watched the unsteady pink goop slowly slide down the wall and into the bookcase. Then everyone started chatting at the same time. The goop was cleaned up, and the party went on until late at night.

In November of that year, I was cast as Red Riding Hood in the Christmas pantomime at Nottingham's Theatre Royal, a historic town in the British Midlands known for its lace, Sherwood Forest, and Robin Hood legend.

Mum and Auntie arrived to assist me in settling in. We put our trailer close to the wall of a large cinema and lived there throughout rehearsals. I moved into a hotel once they went home.

I still needed a chaperone because I was just fifteen, and I believe the leading actress, Cherry Lind, who portrayed Prince Valiant, was instructed to keep an eye on me. Fortunately, she was also staying at the same hotel.

I was the clumsy Red Riding Hood. Tony Heaton played Mother Hubbard (my mother), comic Tony Hancock played Jolly Jenkins, a foolish, well-meaning Baron's page, and variety artists Albert and Les Ward played the Baron's Henchmen. They used guitars, bicycle pumps, washboards, and pretty much anything else to accompany their country-and-western songs. The fairies and woodland creatures were played by Kirby's Flying Ballet. The comedians introduced their own shtick to the show, in classic panto tradition—and, as always, the songs had nothing to do with the tale. I contributed an extremely technical coloratura aria called "The Gypsy and the Bird," which I sang on the way to Grandma's house in the forest. (As a result, I, too, carried my own shtick.)

I was performing this aria one matinée when I became aware of audience laughs. "Oh, Lord!" I exclaimed. My petticoat is most likely falling!" What I didn't realize until I finished the song was that one of the Flying Ballet cables had come undone. The cables were weighted with sandbags and tied off at the side of the stage, and one enormous sandbag had broken free and was swinging over the proscenium on its wire, missing me by inches while I was trilling. I was later told that if I had stepped back just an inch or two, I would have been clobbered.

The cast would occasionally get together after the show. Tony Hancock and his wife frequently hosted at their residence. I knew him from Educating Archie and liked him, despite the fact that we didn't have much in common on the radio show. He was stocky, with a clown's face and wide, sorrowful eyes. Life was always harsh in his humorous routines, and he would stand, staring out at the audience with thick-fingered, "wet fish" hands by his side, trying to grasp the sorrows and tribulations that befell him. He was a miserable alcoholic who eventually committed suicide in real life. But he was well-known even before that tragic event.

I was relieved to return home after Red Riding Hood finished in March 1951.

Chapter 4

Mum was the life and soul of the party that night, and she became absolutely "plotzed" by the size of the Navy rations and the lack of a curfew on board. We must have left the ship at one o'clock in the morning. We got Mum into the tender, but getting her out of the little boat, which was swaying in the swell, was difficult, and I had to push her up the same iron steps I used to push her up.

Auntie held tests for the entire student body once or twice a year. She hired a Royal Academy of Dance examiner to come and test her ballet students, and another examiner came to judge her ballroom students. I was reasonably skilled at ballroom dancing because I went to the studio whenever I could. I was looking forward to competing for my bronze medal, and with Tappets as my partner, I felt the exam would be a breeze.

Unfortunately, the examiner was late. "We've got to go, we've got to go, we'll never make it in time!" Pop kept shouting. My mum was divided between allowing me to take this exam and putting me into the automobile. Pop eventually stated, "We cannot wait any longer." The pleasure of taking the exam was snatched from under my nose by minutes, and I cried and sulked all the way to Morecambe over it. It wasn't anyone's fault, except possibly the examiner's, but it was a heartbreaking moment for me because passing the exam would have done wonders for my ego. Although it was only a bronze medal, I never had another opportunity to take the test.

Charlie Tucker, who had managed both my parents' act and mine since Starlight Roof, arranged all of our engagements. He had a lovely top-floor office on Regent Street. His desk drawers, like a good "dog robber," were supplied with fragrances, nylon stockings, pens, and cufflinks from the United States, which he gave out as favors to his clients. Charlie would give my mother a bottle of perfume or some nylons to take home with her when she came to visit. He once or twice gave me a bottle of Revillon's Carnet de Bal, a lovely perfume that is warm and delicious, and he would periodically slip me a huge, English £5 note. He'd also take us both out to lunch at fancy restaurants like the Caprice or the Savoy. I recall walking alongside him in London and feeling like we were on top of the world; there was no hardship, no misery. Lunch was extraordinary, with clinking china and silverware, soft lighting, pink tablecloths, and attentive waiters—a look into a world that was otherwise out of reach.

In late October of that year, Pop was able to secure three seats for a preview of Rodgers and Hammerstein's South Pacific, starring Mary Martin and Wilbur Evans, as well as as-yet-unknown actors Larry Hagman (who played Yeoman Herbert Quale, Mary Martin's son) and Sean Connery (a mere chorus boy at the time). Everything happened very quickly. "We've got tickets—we're going," Pop remarked, and Mum, Pop, and I set off for a night on the town, which was a rare occurrence in and of itself.

The show was fantastic. What a difference between the cheesiness of vaudeville and a legitimate American musical at Drury Lane's prestigious Theatre Royal. Mary Martin enchanted as Ensign Nellie Forbush, even washing "that man right out of her hair" onstage!

Wilbur Evans, a wonderful baritone, played Emile de Becque opposite her and sang the glorious ballads "Some Enchanted Evening" and "This Nearly Was Mine." The male chorus performed "There Is Nothing Like a Dame" to a standing ovation. There was a large orchestra, and Robert Russell Bennett's musical arrangements were magnificent.

I'll never forget being in the full cinema watching the preview. It took my breath away. I'm also envious. I was also feeling a little hopeless. I assumed I lacked the talent and experience to enter that realm. The show wowed London when it premiered a week later.

Despite being quite busy in 1951, I managed to maintain some sort of a social life. I was still seeing Tony and the Waltons a lot, and if I returned home for the weekends, Mum would take us out for a summer drink to some lovely spot—a club or a tavern on the river.

I would do anything to get home between gigs, even if it meant working twelve hours. I had terrible separation anxiety while I was gone, and I was always worried and wondering. Would my mother be okay? How were the boys doing? I'd go all the way down from the north of England merely to spend one day with the family before returning the next day for another week's work. Whenever I returned home, Mum would do everything she could to make it special. Dingle and Auntie would be there for a large Sunday supper. They'd strive to fill me with affection and attention.

Mum had a hysterectomy about this time. She was away for a few days since she was having a bad time. Pop had started drinking again. Not on a binge, but drinking anyway. I thought I needed to be vigilant and cautious.

Pop attempted to return that night, but was definitely denied entry. He couldn't figure out why the lock had been installed. I'm not sure what I said, except that I needed my privacy. I know the lock made me feel a little safer, even though he could have easily smashed it.

My mother returned, terribly bruised from her surgery. Her muscles were so weak that I assisted her in attempting to ascend the stairs so she could rest in her bedroom. Her legs simply wouldn't support her, and she was really tired. She sat on the stairs, overtaken with sadness, and sobbed. I rushed over to fetch her a cup of tea, and she sat for a time, sipping it slowly, before carefully easing herself back up the remaining steps. My heart broke for her.

My relationship with Pop became more distant than ever after that. He never tried anything else with me again, and I avoided being alone with him at all costs.

But I was conscious that my body was changing: my breasts were growing, my waist was getting smaller, and my legs were getting longer (though still bandy!). When men were near me, I recall being suspicious and cautious. Dingle offered me a big hug, like he frequently did, but it didn't feel right. When I was at Charlie Tucker's office, he offered me a friendly squeeze, and I shrugged him off. Perhaps the interaction with Pop had made an impression.

Fortunately, I became aware of my sense of humor, and I discovered with delight that I could make the family laugh. I'm not sure how I learned I could do it; perhaps it was because I was exposed to vaudeville humor so frequently. Everyone would laugh and smile at my antics and impersonations. It made my brothers feel better, everyone in the family appeared to love it, and it provided me with a new sense of power over my surroundings.

Back in 1951, I was invited to play Princess Balroulbadour, the main girl, in Emile Littler's Christmas pantomime Aladdin at the London Casino. The title part was supposed to be played by Jean Carson.

Aladdin was a lavish production. The Genie's cave at the end of the first act was breathtaking, and the second act had a massive ballet that was masterfully created and executed.

The Olanders, a Danish acrobatic troupe, performed death-defying gymnastics: springboards, leaps, and balancing performances while dressed in silk pantaloons and waistcoats. I had to come down every time they were onstage because they were that excellent. A unique combination of bravado and muscular power, with slender, attractive bodies.

One of the best acrobats was a young man named Fred, who performed twelve incredible butterfly leaps around the stage. He was beautiful, fit (clearly), gentle, and sweet. My mother was aware of my feelings for him and correctly advised, "Bring him down to The Meuse for a weekend." He never stopped swinging from our chandeliers (we didn't have any), she laughed later.

When the show's run ended, I was heartbroken. Fred joined the Olanders on their continued tour of England and Europe. Later that year, I went to watch their act at a theater outside of London with Auntie Gladdy and was able to say hello to him backstage. My heart broke all over again because I knew this was the final time I'd see him.

King George VI died on February 6, 1952. He had been our ruler for sixteen years—nearly my whole life—after reluctantly being crowned following his brother, Edward's, untimely abdication in 1936.

He'd been in poor health for some time. The war had taken its toll, and his frequent smoking had resulted in lung cancer. As her father's health deteriorated, Princess Elizabeth took up more and more of his royal duties. She learned of his death while on the first leg of a Commonwealth visit to Kenya, Australia, and New Zealand. She returned as Queen at the age of twenty-five, having left Britain as a princess.

The play and tour were both done on a tight budget; the costumes were rented, which meant they had all been worn previously. The sets were repurposed from prior productions. The title of the show refers to the growing prominence of television in people's lives, with Look In being a play on the more popular "Listen In" radio tagline.

Because I was touring alone, my mother and, I believe, Charlie Tucker urged Alfred and Paddie to keep an eye on me and take me under their wing. I initially slept on a rollaway cot in the same room as they did. I would go to bed early, and they would return to the motel late. It was challenging for me, and I'm sure it was vexing for them. None of us were pleased with the situation, and I was soon given my own room.

Despite the fact that I was about to turn seventeen, I was still branded as "Britain's youngest singing star," and I was now performing in the show's penultimate place. During this time, I conducted several radio broadcasts and continued the weeks of vaudeville and individual concerts. I had bouts of laryngitis throughout the year—my tonsils were persistently infected—but I didn't worry too much about it and always tried my best to sing through it.

In early September, I got a brief exposure not just to the realm of animated film, but also to the wonderful art of dubbing. The Rose of Baghdad was a Czechoslovakian film from 1949. It was now to be distributed in the United Kingdom, and it presented the story of a lovely singing princess, similar to Aladdin or Ali Baba and the Forty Thieves. A soprano with a beautiful high voice had performed the role of Princess Zeila. The producers requested that I dub the songs into English while recording them with the original orchestrations. I had a coloratura voice, but these songs were so high that, while I managed them, there were several lyrics in the higher register that I battled with.

I wasn't really pleased with the outcome. I didn't believe I had performed well. But when I saw the film, I thought the animation was stunning. I'm glad I completed the work because I don't recall ever dealing with such high-tech material before.

Tony Walton and I kept in touch as much as we could. He had graduated from Radley College that spring and was scheduled to complete his National Service at the end of the summer. I continued to see his gorgeous family, feeling at ease and at ease in their company.

Tony asked me out on our first genuine date in late summer, I suppose. We went to London to see the film The Greatest Show on Earth, which we both liked. Despite the fact that I was approaching the age of seventeen, I was still somewhat gauche, despite my experimentation with Fred. I was inexperienced and introverted, with my social skills falling well behind my ability to trick a huge crowd such as an audience. Tony held my hand at the theater, but I was stiff and withdrawn since I sensed he was getting interested in a deeper connection, something I wasn't ready for. Fortunately, nothing stood in the way of our friendship.

I was cast in yet another holiday pantomime just after my birthday. I portrayed Princess Bettina in the Coventry Hippodrome's production of Jack and the Beanstalk this time. It was yet another lead female part. I was never asked to play the lead male because I was too young and, despite all of my dancing classes, my legs were not strong enough.

Early rehearsals were held in London with renowned choreographer Pauline Grant. Charlie Tucker had requested Pauline to be my mentor, to help me with my demeanor and to give me some West End sass. We became excellent friends, and she had a significant impact on my life. Pauline was petite and packed tight in her skin, with slightly protruding eyes and prettily bowed pouting lips. She reminded me of Leslie Caron. She was a former dancer with wonderful little hands and her feet looked to be situated "at a quarter to three" (my mother's description). She always wore very high heels and donned suits and silk blouses with neck bows to soften the fitted appearance. Every year, if she could afford it, she would buy herself one haute-couture Hardy Amies outfit. She told me that having a few exquisite things in my wardrobe is more important than having a bunch of cheap ones.

The pantomime's primary attraction was comedian Norman Wisdom. He was a mischievous little lad, a wonderful comedian in the style of Charlie Chaplin. He was dressed in a black suit that appeared to be too small for him, with the peak of his cap pushed to the side of his head. He walked weird and played the part of a child pretty effectively. He was married, and his wife seemed to be pregnant all the time during the time I knew him.

Norman and I formed a sort of friendship; we worked well together onstage, and on Saturday nights when he'd travel home (returning on Monday), he'd sometimes give me a lift as far as Ealing, on London's north side, where he lived. My mother or Dingle would drive up from Walton and wait at a particular roundabout. Norman would drop me off, I'd switch cars, and either Mum or Dingle would drive me home.

Pauline Grant stayed with us at the start of the run in Coventry, then returned on occasion—ostensibly to check on us, but actually to see Sam Newsome. His cheerful face would appear at my dressing room door at the most unexpected times, and it was always a delight to see him. He was always cordial, and his manners were impeccable.

Mum and Dad purchased a used car, a Hillman Minx, which I named "Bettina" after my character in the program. It was a lovely small car that was really handy. I didn't drive it, despite the fact that it was technically "my car." It was actually my mother's to use and enjoy, but I was quite happy that I had paid for it with my wages.

I also bought out Pop's portion a year or two later, and the deed of The Meuse was transferred to my name. This increased my sense of obligation to work because it was now entirely my responsibility to make the payments. We would truly perish if I did not contribute. I didn't complain since I knew how much the place meant to my mother, and I had promised her and the rest of the family that I would look after them. I justified working so hard by knowing that I was contributing to the upkeep of our home. The unimaginable threat of losing The Meuse inspired my desire to keep every home I've ever owned afterwards.

Dad, Win, Johnny, Auntie Gladys, Keith, Tappets, and the gang from Auntie's dancing class came up for the final night of Jack and the Beanstalk and assisted with the massive pack-up. Bettina, the automobile, was brought up, and all of my baggage, trunks, makeup, and other belongings were piled into her and another car, until both were completely full.

This was a time of stress and considerable guilt for me. Tony was obviously fond of me and wanted more than I could offer at the time. While I had strong feelings for him, I wanted to see more of life before committing to anyone. I didn't realize how much he meant to me until much later.

That April, I had an important concert at Bournemouth's Winter Garden. I performed with the Bournemouth Symphony Orchestra, conducted by Rudolf Schwarz. The high F above the top C in Mignon's "Polonaise" was the only thing that worried me about my program. During rehearsals, I battled with it. "Don't take the top F, just hold onto the C and come down to the B flat," Maestro Schwarz suggested. It remains appropriate." But I despised the notion. I was known for my high notes, which made me feel like I was cheating and that the finish of my song would be flat and unexciting. It smacked of failure to me.

A few weeks later, I began work on Cap and Belles, another Charlie Tucker extravaganza. The show's title, "The New Laugh, Song, and Dance Show," was a pun on the "cap and bells" used by medieval court jesters. It starred Max Wall (billed as "The Queen's Jester"), who also composed and penned part of the music and lyrics. This time around, I was dubbed "Britain's Youngest Prima Donna." I had two solo performances in the show, the first being a song called "My Heart Is Singing," and the second being "La Dansa," an Italian tarantella that I sang with the help of "Les Belles of the Ballet." I appreciated its intense flavor, but I couldn't understand a word I was singing. I was dressed in a bilious green Spanish gown with a swath of scarlet frills beneath a long train and held a fan. I stamped my feet and twisted my skirt, pushing the red frills aside...For an Italian tune, there's a lot of Spanish attitude!

Max Wall was one of the most gifted and cerebral comedians I'd ever worked with. It wasn't simply that he was good; he exuded a certain aura; he was one of only a few great clowns in my opinion.

Offstage, he was a solemn, somber, and largely absent figure. He gave the sense that he was gloomy and should be left alone. I never saw him jerk his head back in laughter. I never saw him crack a joke. He was devastatingly sharp and humorous onstage, yet there was a wrath in him that he poured into humor.

Our schedule during the summer and autumn of 1953 was nothing short of exhausting. We spent a week in each of more than thirty locations around the United Kingdom.

On a Monday night in a new theater, before the first performance, I'd go up to the wardrobe department and press my clothes, because there wasn't always a wardrobe mistress, and even if there was, she was always swamped with other costumes.

In some towns, the audiences were so raucous that the management turned on the house lights in the balconies to watch what was going on. On a Saturday night in Glasgow, drunks would throw bottles at each other during the second house. I trilled louder than normal onstage, my hands clenched in front of me, belting out my arias over the yelling and fighting.

It never occurred to me that I might be learning particular skills: how to deal with an audience, how to deal with an angry public, how to survive in a theater so densely packed with cigarette smoke that it spiraled down the enormous spotlights onto the stage. ("Do not ever let me hear you complain about smoke affecting your voice!" my mother once warned me.) It had never occurred to me that I was inadvertently acquiring essential tactics from the great vaudevillians I saw night after night. Much later, I would realize that all of my early effort had served me well and had prepared me for everything that was to come.

On June 2, 1953, Queen Elizabeth II was crowned, and all cinemas were closed. London had been beautifully decked for the occasion, with flags flying everywhere and floral garlands draped from lampposts. The coronation event was aired for the first time in history, and there was a fascinating commentary by Richard Dimbleby, a well-known reporter highly respected in England, who had a rich, deep voice: "Here comes Her Majesty now, walking with immense grace, carrying the scepter and orb..."

My family and I watched the event at home and were captivated by it, particularly by the little queen, who wore the hefty seven-pound jeweled crown and sat for hours in her huge white satin embroidered gown. The music was magnificent and motivating, with a full orchestra, massed voices, and fanfares. It was a great event. Her Majesty's speech to the country was extremely affecting; this gorgeous young woman devoted to serving the British people. That night, nearly every peak and hill in Britain had a bonfire burning atop it. My father typically went alone to the crown of Leith Hill and privately pledged fealty to his new queen.

Bettina came to a hissing halt in the middle of the pool after Mum gunned the engine. Her engine was fully flooded. We waded out of the deep water in our finery and staggered to a garage to request that the car be towed to safety. We never made it to the concert.

The majestic and ancient Hampton Court Palace on the Thames was lit up for the coronation and opened to the public. My mother, my father, my brothers, and I went to see it. It was a warm summer evening with a heavy floral aroma in the air. The neighboring river gleamed, reflecting the bright lights. It was incredibly lovely strolling around the exquisite gardens under the stars. Everyone seems to have a companion. I wished I could share it with someone.

Tony was in Canada, and despite the fact that he wrote almost every day, I think I missed him more than ever before. Because it was such a gorgeous English summer night, the recollection of that evening in Hampton Court is still burning in my mind today. I couldn't face the thought that someone with Tony's sense wasn't seeing and sharing it with me.

Chapter 5

During the Cap and Belles tour, I began to have significant reservations about my future chances. I began to consider what I truly had to offer, what I'd learned, and what I aspired to accomplish. I was seventeen now, still traveling indefinitely and singing the same songs night after night. My youthful "freak" voice appeared to be changing, and I was concerned about my attraction if I lost that gimmick.

The theater is quite prestigious and has a long history. It was the crown jewel of the Moss Empires Corporation. Almost every major American performer has appeared at the Palladium. It seats over 2,000 people, but standing on the stage, one feels as if they can touch the entire audience. It's spotless, unlike the gaudy vaudeville theaters I'd been playing in. It is also the best place in London to view a pantomime.

Everything about the 1953/1954 Cinderella staging was elegant. The show was spectacular, and the outfits were cutting-edge. The staging was done by Charles Henry, who was also involved in Starlight Roof, while the choreography was done by Pauline Grant.

The show's production qualities were excellent, with circling stages and actual white ponies pulling the magnificently gilded vehicle. (The ponies were adorable, but they had an uncanny ability to take a poop on stage whenever I had friends in the crowd.) The Fairy Godmother performed a magnificent transformation sequence, allowing Cinderella to attend the ball. My crinoline was so large in the grand finale wedding sequence that I had to arrive backstage dressed in my bodice, sleeves, and petticoat and walk into the crinoline skirt, which was supported on a stand because it was so bejeweled and unwieldy. The troupe, Prince Charming, and I were carried up from below stage on a hydraulic lift for the climactic tableau, which included a shining white set and costumes.

Cinderella was a huge success, and we received rave reviews. "Julie, this is the perfect part for you at the perfect age," my mother commented after the opening night. It couldn't have happened to you at a better time in your career." From December through March, I did two concerts a day, and I enjoyed every minute of it.

Sandy Wilson's musical production The Boy Friend, written and composed by Wilson, was a huge hit in London. Because of my own performing schedule, I hadn't been able to watch the show, but it had been playing to immense acclaim and success—so much so that two American producers, Cy Feuer and Ernest Martin, purchased the rights for Broadway. They were famous for blockbuster smashes like Guys and Dolls and Can-Can. Feuer and Martin opted to build a whole new company for the Broadway play because the London producers refused to release any of their skilled cast members.

Charlie Tucker said that Vida Hope, the director of The Boy Friend, will be attending an afternoon performance of Cinderella. Later, I discovered that Hattie Jacques, the sweet comedian from Educating Archie, had suggested to Vida that she check out the young lead at the Palladium. Vida was accompanied to the theater by Sandy Wilson. The next thing I know, I was surprised with a two-year contract to portray Polly Browne in The Boy Friend on Broadway. I'm not sure if Hattie recognized how important she was to me.

I made my choice. For the first time in my life, I dug in my heels and told Charlie Tucker, "I cannot do it for two years, but I will do it for one." Charlie was shocked and told me I couldn't dictate to the American producers in that manner. But I was resolute, and exclaimed, "Look, I don't care! It's fine if they don't want me." I guess I thought that my demand on a one-year contract rather than a two-year deal would cause Messrs. Feuer and Martin to decline their offer. They agreed to my terms, much to my astonishment.

Cinderella's run ended in March, and I wasn't supposed to depart for America until August. In the meantime, Charlie Tucker informed me that he had an offer for me to portray an American girl from the South in a new "play with music" called Mountain Fire. I had always wanted to explore legitimate theater, and now I was being asked to perform in one. "Legit" at long last!

In their Kensington apartment, I met the director, Peter Cotes, and his wife, Joan Miller. I believe they recruited me because I was the appropriate age and sufficiently nubile—certainly not because of my Southern accent, which was, to put it mildly, horrible.

The drama, set in Tennessee's mountains, was a dark, tragic allegory based on the biblical account of Sodom and Gomorrah. Bill Birney and Howard Richardson, who previously wrote the hugely successful Dark of the Moon, wrote it.

I started working on my role with Joan Miller. She attempted to assist me in finding the nuances required for the role, but, as with sad music and the horrible screen test, the emotions overpowered me. Every day, streams of tears flowed. I was dreading going to work.

Gillian Lynne, the now-famous choreographer of such hits as Cats and The Phantom of the Opera, appeared in the show as a young, wanton girl. Jerry Wayne, who portrayed the traveling salesman who captivated my character, Becky, was gorgeous, but he was on a health craze at the time, and he ate garlic till it came out of his ears.

His clothes, breath, hair, everything stank—and we were having love scenes together. Someone informed me that if you eat garlic for self-defense, you don't notice it on others, so I started eating a lot of garlic myself. It made little difference except to keep other members of the company at a safe distance from us both.

Stefan de Haan, a delightful man around fifteen years my senior who also functioned as our musical director, composed the music. He was European, intellectual, shy, and entertaining. Our director couldn't decide whether the orchestra should be in the pit, offstage, or not at all. After all, this was a play, so he reasoned that one instrument, a guitar, would suffice. Every night, we tried a new approach to the show.

Neil, Stefan, Aunt Joan, and I took a short vacation together after the performance ended in July. We chartered a small river boat and sailed up the Thames. Auntie and Stefan got along great, and she became Neil and my unspoken chaperone. We formed a good foursome.

My period suddenly and unexpectedly began with a vengeance on the train down to Southampton. I felt mortified—and perhaps a little relieved. Neil and I shared a bed for the night, but it was strictly platonic. It must have been excruciatingly frustrating for him. He promised to come down to see me when I got to New York. He boarded his ship the next morning, and I waved until he was out of sight...Then it was back to Walton-on-Thames on the lonely train.

My mum was not at home when I arrived. She might have been annoyed with me and opted not to be there when I returned. She could have simply gone to the pub for a drink. Whatever the case, the home was depressingly empty, I was unhappy and sorry for myself, and I went to lie down on my bed. Mum eventually arrived and went to find me. She sobbed with relief when I informed her Neil and I had not completed our relationship. The great migration to America began.

I was supposed to fly to America in three days and had a lot of packing to do, but I was rushed into Dad's car with Donald, Chris, and Mum. Auntie was in poor health, but she was with Dingle. I had no idea where they went that weekend.

Pop had been working himself up for days, his wrath rising to the surface and ready to burst. It could have been a coincidence that he acted out just as I was about to leave, but he must have noticed how much attention I was getting. Pop, on the other hand, had no career in vaudeville and was not doing well as a cash register salesman. Auntie and Dingle's presence on our property drove him insane; the dancing lessons in the garden studio irritated him, my mother's support of my aunt and indifference of him...He probably believed he didn't have any friends or a place to call his own in the world. He was, of course, an alcoholic. We later noticed bottles of scotch and vodka strewn throughout the house.

Mum discovered that he had placed an ad in a "lonely hearts" magazine looking for a dinner companion. When she inquired how he could do something like that, he explained that it wasn't for sex, but for company. I'm not sure if that was true, but it was heartbreaking and rocked my mother's world for a long time.

Suffice needless to say, my trip to America was a nightmare. Everyone wanted me to board that plane bound for the United States. My mother, father, Aunt Joan, Dingle, Auntie Gladdy, Charlie Tucker, Johnny, Don, and Chris all came to see me off at Northolt Airport. It was torture saying goodbye. Mum and Auntie were stoic, assuring me not to worry and that everything would be alright. Go!

I recall seeing the plane's massive engines warming up on the tarmac. We were gathered in a sort of army Nissen hut that served as the Northolt passenger holding area. In the dead of night, I walked across the pavement and up the steps to board the massive four-engine Constellation for my first transatlantic flight.

I hadn't yet met any of my coworkers who were also flying to America on the same trip. Everyone was giddy with anticipation, wondering what was ahead for us overseas. I attempted to blend in, but I was preoccupied. I sat next to Dilys Laye, the young actress who would play Dulcie in the musical, and she seemed worldly, serene, and unconcerned. She was an enjoyable company. We decided to attempt to room together on the journey. We had a sleepless night driving from London to New York, stopping for gas in Gander, Newfoundland.

The trip took around eighteen hours, and by the time we arrived in that magnificent city, I was drained physically and mentally. I couldn't take my mind off the family. Will Mum be able to hold out? Will she go through with her divorce from Pop? What would become of the house if she did so? What would she do? Will Don and Chris be okay? My Boy Friend's pay was going to be low. I intended to send half of it home, but would it be enough for them and leave enough for me to live on each week?

I was still struggling with my character, Polly Browne, and figuring out who she was and what I was meant to be doing. I observed everyone else and attempted to imitate them. I had no notion how to study a role or how to "break down" a screenplay. Vida couldn't be of much assistance because she was so preoccupied with the entire production. We weren't going out of town for a tryout run; instead, we were going to open cold on Broadway because the show was already well-known. With so little time to prepare, every day, every rehearsal counted.

To our surprise and despair, word spread around the group that Sandy and Vida had been fired and were no longer permitted to enter the theater. Cy was supposed to take over the show. Something had obviously occurred after hours that we were all unaware of, and the firm was concerned.

I understood Cy was giving me the answers I needed, that he was throwing me the rope I needed. I grabbed it with both hands, and everything fell into place with startling clarity. Thank God for his direction. That night, I portrayed Polly Browne how I believe she should be portrayed: as an innocent, fragile little rich girl who wants nothing more than to be loved for herself.

It was September 30, 1954, the night before my nineteenth birthday, and I'll never forget that performance. The orchestra was fantastic, the company was fantastic, and every chuckle I wished for came my way. The final reception was incredible. The audience erupted in unison, stomping and cheering. As they exited the theater, many danced the Charleston along the aisles.

Backstage, there was a huge, raucous, and enthusiastic crush. On the stage door phone, I attempted to contact my mother in England. Bill Birney, one of Mountain Fire's authors, had invited me out to dinner, and not knowing the customs of a Broadway premiere, I agreed. Everyone else went to Sardi's to wait for the reports, while I went to the Ambassador restaurant with Bill and had a formal and exquisite supper. We eventually arrived at Sardi's, where the maître d' informed us that the group had congregated in an upstairs room. People were waving newspapers or reading reviews. Dilys received fantastic compliments, as did I, miraculously. The Boy Friend was a huge success.

The actual job began after the concert began. We had to record the cast album right away, so we didn't have much time to catch our breath. Every major newspaper and magazine wanted to shoot their own photo layouts and center spreads. These were always completed following the evening show. It was almost like doing an extra show, and we frequently worked late into the night. It was taxing, especially with matinees.

Dilys and I combined our resources and relocated from the Piccadilly Hotel to a one-bedroom apartment at the Hotel Park Chambers on West 58th Street. There was a living area, a closet-sized kitchen with a tiny fridge, hot plate, and sink, a twin-bed bedroom, and a bathroom.

It was in a decent position, and there was a good drugstore across the street with a soda fountain. It was bliss compared to Piccadilly. We didn't have much space in our wardrobes or our one bathroom, but we managed.

Everything about New York seemed to be an assault at first. The pace, the customs, the stress of being in a fantastic hit show, the exposure to so much fresh and interesting. There were days when I was so overwhelmed that I had to pause at shop entrances to catch my breath.

My weekly income was $450. Almost half of it was deducted for taxes, and the remainder was used to send $150 home. It left me with around $75 per week to cover the Park Chambers and meals. Dilys and I were generally absolutely broke by Thursday, with very little to eat in our tiny kitchen.

Eleanor Lambert (considered the founder of fashion PR and the creator of the "International Best Dressed List" in 1940) arranged for me to design a fashion layout for a magazine. I modeled numerous outfits that fit me perfectly, and she later gave them to me. I objected, but she responded, "No, no, you used them; please take them." I couldn't have been happier.

Lou Wilson was a frequent guest at the Park Chambers Hotel. If it was convenient, he'd come over after the concert for a cup of tea and we'd just sit on the couch and speak. We talked about Charlie Tucker, my parents, his divorce, and his little daughter "Tuppence," whom he didn't see very often. I believe he felt lonely as well.

She and I decided that because he had been so good, we would cook him dinner one night. We wondered what we could make with our two-burner stove. We couldn't possibly afford to take him out to eat. I went out and purchased a can of Dinty Moore Beef Stew, which we diligently boiled and served. He was courteous and ate every bite. But then he politely asked how much money we had, individually and collectively.

When Neil was in Canada, we had nightly phone chats that grew longer and longer over time. "Julie, you simply have to cut down on your long distance bill," Lou would advise. But, as lovers do, we talked for an hour or more, and the minutes passed.

To my astonishment, Neil became worried and controlling, demanding that I account for where I'd been and what I'd done. Sometimes he didn't believe my replies, and we'd have angry phone conversations. "Neil, why do you doubt what I'm saying?" I'd protest, but he'd still pump me. It was strange and eventually irritated me. I attempted to keep our chats short at times, but it only made him suspicious. In the relationship, I began to feel claustrophobic.

Other amusing incidents occurred. In the show, Tony and Polly are about to kiss when Hortense, the maid, comes in and interrupts them. The actor who played Hortense once missed her cue. As we leaned in for the kiss, John Hewer and I exchanged glances. We leaned in further, pecked quietly, and then broke apart, not knowing what else to do. Hortense is still missing. After a long pause, I exclaimed, "Well, I have to go now!" and left poor John standing there. For months following that, he teased me about it. As I moved away, I could hear the actress's footsteps running toward the stage.

Our lease on the sublet expired, and Dilys and I moved to a much nicer apartment on 57th Street, close to the East River, with two bedrooms. Dilys arrived one night with Michael Kidd, the famed choreographer of the film Seven Brides for Seven Brothers and the Broadway performances of Finian's Rainbow, Guys and Dolls, and Can-Can. Everyone was excited to meet Michael Kidd. He just sat in the middle of us, conversing amiably, seemingly ignorant of his stature. He was adorable—attractive, humorous, and full of life.

Dilys' mother moved in with us. She was as gregarious as Dilys, and often battled with her daughter for Dilys' friends' attention. Dilys would scream at her mother one minute, then defend her the next, and was frequently brought to tears. My heart broke for Dilys, who was, to put it mildly, a tough lady. I started to feel down. The woman was in our flat, in my life, in my face, and she was ruining everything for all of us. I pondered getting a place of my own, but I couldn't afford it.

Dilys and her mother miraculously chose to leave, and Millie Martin moved in with me instead. Dilys and I are still friends, but Millie and I were easy and agreeable housemates who became wonderful friends.

Chapter 6

My boy companion was a huge learning experience for me. Working for a year on one job allowed me to put myself to the test night after night. I learnt how to establish the show's hilarious moments and the importance of being authentic when acting comedy.

Madame Stiles-Allen had taught me how to strengthen the note before a troublesome note in a tune. I was astounded and humbled to learn that this technique can be used in many different parts of theater, including drama, comedy, song, and dance. It appears to me that if a performance moment is lost, it helps to look at the instant preceding it—to help build up and strengthen the troubled area. That year on Broadway taught me some of the most valuable lessons of my life.

A few days later, I was asked to meet composer Frederick (Fritz) Loewe. Mr. Loewe was the polar opposite of Mr. Lerner, who appeared convoluted and difficult to understand. He was the oldest of the two and exuded Viennese elegance. He greeted me with a friendly smile and kissed my hand gallantly.

Soon after, I was approached to audition for the renowned Richard Rodgers, who was casting his and Oscar Hammerstein's new production, Pipe Dream. I took Lou Wilson to a theater and handed the pianist my audition piece, "The Waltz Song" by Tom Jones. I'd been requested to sing something other than a song from The Boy Friend...something more vocally difficult.

I had no idea at the time that I was about to embark on one of the most challenging, magnificent, and complex experiences of my life, or that I would be led through the perilous jungle of self-discovery by several of the nicest, most intelligent giants one could ever expect to meet. However, I am getting ahead of myself.

I was feeling a little better by the time we arrived in London. My family was overjoyed to see me, and we had a wonderful day telling stories and chatting with everyone. It was wonderful to see my siblings. Mum and Pop were actually reunited, though I don't recall seeing much of him. He might have kept his distance—and I was surely preoccupied.

Tony Walton had returned to the United States from Canada in late 1954. Following that, he studied at the Slade School of Art in London while still working part-time at the Wimbledon Theatre, giving him a perfect blend of idealistic instruction as well as the fundamentals—the nuts and bolts of practical theater.

Tony exuded a sense of security, of being known and cherished. It was a big comfort to be close to someone I knew—and who knew me—so well after the turmoil of the year in America and the seesawing relationship with Neil.

The journey to L.A. was pleasant enough, but it was a strange point in my life, almost a pause. Lou Wilson had intended to accompany me, but he would not be able to arrive until a few days after my arrival.

Arthur Schwartz and his wife welcomed me into their home. They couldn't have been nicer, treating me like a young protégée about to be launched into a world of waiting. They wanted to show me off and introduce me to as many people as possible who could boost my career. They hosted a meal for me at their Beverly Hills home. It was a large gathering, and I was requested to sing a couple of High Tor songs. Arthur performed for me, and despite my shyness, everyone was nice and pleased.

In his wonderful autobiography, The Street Where I Live, Alan Jay Lerner writes that most of the cast of My Fair Lady planned to arrive in New York a week before the start of rehearsals on January 3, but I waited until the last minute because I'd had so little time with my family since returning from The Boy Friend in September. Alan had no idea why I insisted on the delay, but I needed to be home for the holidays, especially for Don and Chris.

I sobbed as our plane lifted off, as if my heart would burst. Lou appeared perplexed at first, then anxious. I sat alongside him, sobbing uncontrollably. I couldn't explain why and couldn't stop myself. It was an emotional tidal wave.

By the time we began rehearsals in 1956, both theaters were in disrepair; the larger one had been converted into a cinema. The upstairs was never used, run-down, dusty, an old vacant area, yet the small stage and traces of the catwalk remained. However, it provided us with enough space to get the show up and running, as well as some seats on the floor for the creative team to view rehearsals. It also provided us with perfect privacy. I assume we were the first to use it after it had been closed for so long. Since then, it has been brilliantly renovated by the Disney Company and serves as the focal point of the revitalization of 42nd Street.

So I arrived at Moss Hart. Moss Hart, the legendary director of My Fair Lady and subsequently Camelot. The man responsible for Winged Victory and Lady in the Dark with Gertrude Lawrence; the man who collaborated with Irving Berlin, Cole Porter, Richard Rodgers, Kurt Weill, and wrote the screenplays for Gentleman's Agreement and the original A Star Is Born, to name a few of his many accomplishments.

Moss' aura was enticing, his intelligence smart and keen, and his personality appealing. He was a one-of-a-kind and captivating individual. He walked with a slight stoop in the "earth shoes" he had specifically manufactured for him during rehearsals. He frequently clasped a pipe between his teeth, although it was never lit, as far as I knew. He liked vintage cufflinks and sported a gold signet ring. He was pleasant, witty, and accepted everyone. He did, in fact, embrace the world and all that it had to offer.

I had to wear one outfit over another at one point during the show to prepare for a quick change between scenes. When Eliza returns from the spectacular ball, she is wearing a full-length black velvet cape, and one assumes she is wearing her ball gown beneath it, but I was actually underdressed in a yellow suit skirt and shirt. Eliza storms away after a heated dispute with Higgins. There is just enough time in the rapid scene change to put on the suit jacket and shoes, as well as a new hairpiece and hat for the scene that follows.

The Helene Pons Studio was on the twelfth floor of a skyscraper, and the building rocked violently whenever there was a strong wind. I was fitting the yellow suit and the velvet coat on top of it one day in early February. Beaton was a taskmaster, and I'd been standing on a small dais for a long time while the hemlines were marked and the cloak was pinned. Several seamstresses had jostled and poked me. The structure began to tremble, and I grew terribly hot. Then I started swaying, and I knew I was ready to pass out. I was sweating and had to lie down on Helene's couch. Beaton was unconcerned.

When I felt he was being condescending or uninterested, I began to taunt him a little, utilizing my budding cockney accent to good effect. And he enjoyed it! When I purposefully displayed a lower-class demeanor, I could see the tiniest crack of a smile on his pursed lips and a little glint in his eye. I believe we eventually came to respect each other, and his magnificent clothes made one forget about anything else.

I watched the original Pygmalion film several times with Wendy Hiller and Leslie Howard, looking for clues to help me with this character. I still hadn't mastered the cockney accent, and I'm not sure if I ever did. I quickly adjusted to the tunes, and I honestly believe I would have been rejected and sent home if it hadn't been for them. I'd heard about people getting fired on the spot and replaced, and I dreaded that humiliation.

Rex's icy and ungenerous demeanor gave me the impression that I wasn't making inroads with him and that he was, quite rightfully, making a fuss about this dumb little English girl who couldn't handle the part. He allegedly once said, "If you don't get rid of that c—, you won't have a show." Thankfully, I was unaware of the remark for many years.

I worried if Moss would have time to pay attention to me. Did he realize how badly I needed direction? I was a blank slate staring out at the world, with no knowledge, assurance, or opinion, and no idea how to develop a character, shape it, mold it, and bring it to life. It would have been nice to have an idea, right or wrong, but I didn't have anything to draw upon. I was inexperienced, and it was painfully obvious to me. The only thing I felt was something inside of me—some knowledge of "smarts" and a desire to be set free. If only someone could gently untangle the knotted ball of string in my gut and pull it up and out of my head, I could be Eliza, locate and comprehend her.

On the way to rehearsals that fateful Saturday, I felt like I was on my way to the dentist with a severe toothache. You dread the experience, but things have progressed to the point that you must deal with the discomfort. You hope to feel better after it's over.

"Julie, you and I have some work to do, but there isn't much time for niceties," Moss stated to me. If we are to accomplish anything, this will be painful and tough." I knew his words were selected with care and decency, and I readied myself for whatever lay next.

We ran through the entire show with the principals on Monday morning. I knew Rex and everyone else were keeping an eye on me to see what the weekend had produced. I definitely lost behind 50% due to nerves, but I also gained 50%, and I was on my way from there. Rex appeared to be at ease.

I was now able to build on the basis Moss had laid for me, and I gradually entrenched the job. As my confidence grew, I began to add my own flourishes and touches. But I never stopped working on Eliza for the entire two years I was on Broadway. She's such a character, and I've never had a better acting lesson than the one Moss gave me that weekend.

We went to New Haven to get the performance started. Our theater, the Shubert, was practically next door to the hotel where the majority of the company's members were staying.

The weather was terrible—snowy, blustery, and freezing—and we were trapped indoors by the out-of-town craziness that comes with putting on a major show. Oliver Smith's sets were fantastic, but his designs required two big turntables, which were the torment of Biff's, Moss', and the company's lives because they were slow and cumbersome and rarely lined up properly.

Rex's rehearsals in New Haven were a nightmare. Kitty had warned Moss that singing with the orchestra would take Rex off his feet—and it did, because he couldn't hear his melodies, everything sounded different, and he had no idea where his cues were. Franz Allers worked almost exclusively with him, but Rex was terrified and caused quite a commotion.

On February 4, 1956, we formally opened our doors in New Haven. I got to my hotel room in the late afternoon, just before the show, and in my mailbox was a hefty envelope with a short message from Moss: "Darling Julie, I think these belong more to you than to me."

Inside were two metal discs—a pair of Covent Garden Opera House ticket tokens Moss had found many years ago and fashioned into cufflinks. When one had a box at the opera, one produced a token and was directed to the right seat.

I was almost brought to my knees by the gift. It was incredibly touching and appropriate. Not only were the tokens from my own country and the famous opera theater in our play included, but they were also from Moss, and I knew how much he cherished them. The fact that he chose to give them to me was the highest honor I could have hoped for. I still treasure them to this day.

On opening night in New York City, I felt like a prizefighter entering the ring; I was the right weight, I knew what I had to do, my voice had returned, and I was as prepared as I could be. That was the only time in my entire stage career that I felt like that.

Thomas W. Lamb designed the Hellinger Theater on West 51st Street in the 1930s as a Warner Bros. movie palace. Our producer,

Herman Levin, took a risk when he chose the theater as a home for My Fair Lady, as it had previously been a bit of a white elephant and was located a few streets uptown from the main Broadway area. But it was a lovely theater, especially the front inside of the building, with an amazing lobby that perfectly matched the sophistication of our presentation. Though a little narrow backstage, it was one of the largest and best-equipped New York theaters, with a seating capacity of 1800 people.

Later, in 1970, the Dutch bought it, but after a run of failures, they leased it and eventually sold it to the Times Square Church in 1989. In the years afterwards, many parties have attempted to restore the building as a legitimate theater, but to no avail—which is very unfortunate, because Broadway must and should retain every great theater that it can.

On March 15, 1956, My Fair Lady premiered. We only had one paid preview after further tech rehearsals, which the crowd positively accepted. Moss assembled the cast onstage before the curtain went up on opening night. He gave us a short, delightful speech in which he told us that we were all wonderful and that if the audience didn't enjoy the play, well, what did they know? "I have only one thing left to say: God bless us all...and screw Tiny Tim," he continued.

The next three months of the run are pure pleasure; fleshing out the part, giving it your all, playing with it, and discovering depth. During the next three months, one looks for anything to hold one's attention: listening to countermelodies in the orchestra that one has never heard before, revising a line for better effect, or discovering something new. The last three months have been a slog: everything you can think of to concentrate, be disciplined, and apply all you've learned. And I still had another year to go!

Tickets to the show appeared to be worth gold dust overnight. The advance sales were phenomenal. We learned that a couple had received a pair of tickets in the mail anonymously. Despite the fact that they had no idea who had delivered them, they opted to accept the wonderful present. They went to the theater, had a great time, and then returned home to find their house had been broken into. The intruders had left a message that said, "Hope you enjoyed the show." If you think about it, it's quite inventive!

One night, a fraying rope holding a flat stored in the fly of the theater snapped. The massive piece of scenery swung sideways, then plummeted at an angle, skewering the stage with a thunderous thud directly below Rex's painted scrim. The draft caused the scrim to bulge forward, splinters and debris spilling out beneath it.

It just so happened that no one was backstage at this time, due to Rex's injunction that the scenery not be touched. It was a miracle that no one was wounded. But the impact was horrifyingly loud, and the orchestra and Rex came to a halt—then, with wonderful foresight, he exclaimed to Franz Allers, "Well, come on, come on—give me that bit with the 'clarionet.'" The audience applauded, the show resumed, stage managers quickly cleared the shattered set behind the drop, and we finished the show.

From a lofty desk in the wings, Biff Life called the show. He'd stand there wearing headphones, cuing the lights, sound, and environment. If I had a chance, I would offer him a hug, and he would acknowledge me with a nod and a smile as he went about his business. While he was distracted, I would gently remove his tie clip or steal his money from his back pocket. Later, he'd pretend to look for it, and I'd appear out of nowhere. I'm sure he caught on soon, but he let me play the foolish game anyhow.

Cathleen Nesbitt, who played Henry Higgins' mother, was a graceful and beautiful woman. She had actually appeared in a minor role in the 1938 film adaptation of Pygmalion. In the show, Beaton had dressed her magnificently, with frills around her wrists and gloves on her hands. You'd never think she had rheumatoid arthritis, which she had for years. Rupert Brooke, the poet who died tragically in the First World War, had been her great love. She frequently mentioned him.

"Oh, if only Rupert and I had had that opportunity!" she exclaimed when she learned about the Dictabelts Tony and I sent each other. I'd still have him with me."

In the early spring, my mother visited New York. She came over with Charles Tucker, and it was a delight to indulge her and attempt to make her happy.

I don't remember her reaction to seeing me in My Fair Lady. I'm sure she enjoyed the show, but I don't recall any embraces of excitement or pride in my accomplishment. Looking back, I believe she was tired, befuddled, and absent; perhaps because she was seeing New York for the first time, but more likely as a result of the tension at home.

approximately five months into the run, I began to observe that, while I would begin the show in good voice, my vocal quality would deteriorate approximately two-thirds of the way through the evening. After a few weeks, my voice would endure about half the concert before losing strength and sounded fainter. My vocal strength lasted only a quarter of the way through the show after a few more weeks. It was perplexing and disturbing; I had never encountered anything like it before.

I spoke my way through "The Rain in Spain," thinking to myself, "In one minute, I'll be as mortified as I've ever been in my entire life." I didn't have the courage to stand in front of the audience and apologize. "I've also lost my voice." I knew I couldn't stop a show, break character, and chat to the audience without management's permission, and I knew I couldn't sing "I Could Have Danced All Night" as a talk-song. It's all about the melody, with a big, soaring finish.

Dr. Rexford, an Austrian, old-school, competent throat doctor, eventually saw me. "No wonder you're having problems," he stated after one look at my cables. You're suffering from severe vocal fatigue. If you hop on one leg for the greatest period of time, it will eventually weaken. If you rest it overnight, it may feel a bit better the next day, but if you ride it again the next day, it will become weaker sooner. That's what's been going on with your wires."

Dr. Rexford advised ten days of rest, and my father arrived at the same time. It was tough for me since I wanted to make him happy, but I had to rest and be silent. I was a wreck of nervousness, anxiety, and tension, knowing that so much of the show depended on me. I knew I needed to get back to performing as soon as possible, despite the fact that I still had more than a year left on my contract.

I started going to see Dr. Rexford every Saturday morning. He'd examine my vocal chords by pulling my tongue out so far that I became an expert at relaxing my muscles and rarely gagged at the mirror halfway down my throat. He always gave me a vitamin shot— B-12 and B-Complex—which was excruciatingly painful because he insisted on preserving his old needles and resterilizing them, which rendered them incredibly dull. He'd then sit at his piano and force me to sing along with him. He used a horrible falsetto voice to vocally demonstrate what he wanted from me, but he knew his craft.

Doing two strong gigs on the same day can leave you exhausted. I'd gradually resurrect myself for the Thursday evening performance, and by Friday night, I'd feel a little better. Saturday arrived, and with two more gigs, I'd be flattened once again. On Sunday, I could relax, but by Monday evening, we had restarted the process.

The New York docks are located at the bottom of 51st Street on the Hudson River, and the Queen Mary or Queen Elizabeth Cunard liners departed for England at noon on a Wednesday. I'd be in my dressing room, getting ready for the day's first show, when I'd hear the enormous ship's horn as the tugboats guided one or the other out to sea. I was always unhappy when I heard that. I yearned to be aboard and sailing away in the fresh sea air, since the liners meant freedom and home.

For some reason, about three months after we opened, I began to laugh onstage. I have no idea what motivated this heinous lack of discipline, but I couldn't stop myself. When this happened, Rex would glance at me in complete amazement, his eyebrows arched high, and I giggled even more out of nervousness. I'm ashamed to admit that there were moments when I couldn't even speak my lines. I coped very well if I didn't look at Rex, but he was so unpredictable with his reactions and what he may do that the minute I stepped onstage with him, the simplest thing would send me off. I can only speculate on how frayed my nerves were. Was Rex playing me? Did he detect my admiration and dread of him? Did I pick up on his displeasure with me? Nobody knows!

"The rain in Spain" was a memorable scene in My Fair Lady. Eliza has finally spoken flawlessly, and everyone is ecstatic. Pickering pretends to be a bull and charges the cloak, then Higgins swirls Eliza in his arms for a mad tango, at the end of which they all fall back onto the couch with laughter. Applause usually ended the show at this point, and there was time for a quick sotto voce exchange between Rex, Coote, and me.

Chapter 7

My twenty-first birthday was in October of the first year of My Fair Lady. Charlie Tucker, my mother, and my girlfriend Susan Barker all flew over for it. Charlie threw an after-theater birthday dinner upstairs at the legendary 21 Club. Lou Wilson, Rex and Kay, "Cooter," and Cathleen were all present. Of course, Stanley and his wife were invited, as it was also his birthday.

When I reviewed the agreement with Lou Wilson later, I saw that Charlie had increased his already high commission by a significant amount. Lou was furious, and I felt betrayed. I had signed the paper, so the damage was done, but that incident had permanently altered the tone of Charlie and my relationship.

Tony and I settled into a more peaceful way of life after they left. He couldn't work technically because he had to wait to take the United Scenic Artists of America exam in order to join the union, and that exam was only given once a year. He started looking for work nevertheless.

His passion was theater, and our amazing set designer, Oliver Smith, was really sympathetic to him. Tony's portfolio impressed him, so he invited him to his Brooklyn Heights home and counseled him on the theater, the union, and how to proceed.

Many years later, I realized that I had very low blood sugar and that the only thing that kept me going under stress was adrenaline. I ultimately compensated for this by eating high-protein meals and sipping liquid protein during the show. It made a huge difference in my energy and stability, and I wish I had known more about it back then.

Tony and I went to watch West Side Story's Actors' Fund Benefit, which was our main opponent. From the first downbeat of the overture to the final note of the evening, it was a marvel of a show. West Side Story was to song and dance what My Fair Lady was to music and book. Both series were titans in their own right. Chita Rivera, who portrayed Anita, and her lover, Tony Mordente (who eventually became her husband), as well as Carol Lawrence, who played Maria, became friends.

Two Noel Coward shows were in the works at the same time, and auditions for both were held in the same theater. The great master would sit in the center of the auditorium, with one production company to his left and another to his right. The auditions manager would walk onstage and announce, "This gentleman is auditioning for..."

Tony taught me so much about the theater. I'd complain about Beaton's big hats and the forced perspective of the sets, which made it difficult to navigate through entrances and tiny areas. Tony would gently explain that there is only so much space on stage, and that false perspective is quite necessary, in fact, a component of practically every theatrical design. Stages are frequently raked, couches and beds are foreshortened, and doorways and rooftops are considerably smaller than audiences may expect to see from the theater. As I witnessed Tony at work throughout the years, I came to value the designer's craft.

In July and November of 1956, I appeared twice on The Ed Sullivan Show, the most popular weekly variety show on television at the time. Because Sullivan's ratings were so high, he drew elite performers from all around the world.

I had a brief cameo with Rex in a television program called Crescendo. It had a fantastic cast, including Ethel Merman, Peggy Lee, Benny Goodman, Diahann Carroll, and the great Louis Armstrong. Our paths momentarily intersected. I had finished my piece, and Louis was just getting started. His vitality looked limitless. He clutched the famous trumpet, wiped his brow with a large white handkerchief, and smirked at me. "I saw you in that My Fair Alligator," he murmured with a lovely growl. It all made great sense to me.

In 1957, I released two vinyl albums. One for Angel Records was Tell It Again, a collection of strange children's songs penned and orchestrated by a blind eccentric named "Moondog." He was the American version of an English "busker," performing on the corner of 54th Street and Broadway. He was intelligent, hilarious, and a little intimidating, thanks to his long beard and outfit of flowing robes, open toed sandals, and a Viking's helmet. He also had a spear. He wasn't insane, but he was clearly unique. His music was refined and distinctive. Some of his rhythms were in five-fourths and seven-eighths, which I found difficult to sing because I had never sung them before. Martyn Green, well-known for his Gilbert and Sullivan performances, gave me the album.

The Lass with the Delicate Air was the title of my second album for RCA Records that year. The arranger/conductor was Irwin Kostal, and it marked the start of a long cooperation. We collaborated on another CD, and he later worked as an arranger/conductor on the films Mary Poppins and The Sound of Music. The Lass with the Delicate Air was a collection of English ballads, and while I believe RCA thought I would choose more popular songs, I was eager to record the songs because I knew there would come a day when these charming little classics would not be as easy for me to sing.

I thought the tunes were lovely. I adored the ballad "In My Own Little Corner," as well as the tune "Impossible," which I sang with Edie Adams.

Edie exuded a dazzling warmth about her. At the time, she was dating the legendary comedian Ernie Kovacs, with whom she later married.

Kaye Ballard and Alice Ghostley were excellent foils for one another. Kaye's character was forceful and authoritative, whereas Alice's was goofy and giggly. Jon Cypher was attractive and had a decent singing voice.

It felt intimidating to watch live television. We were performing a musical show, but unlike in theater, there were cameras doing a slow dance around us at all times (and they were much bigger back then); people were pulling cables out of the way, and we were trying to ignore all the chaos of a working crew while convincing our audience that there was no one around but us actors. Joe Papp was quite helpful in this regard, as he seamlessly controlled traffic on the floor, cued the performers in terms of where we needed to be, how long before we were on camera, and which camera was being used.

The most challenging sequence for me was the transformation scene, in which Cinderella is dressed in rags one moment and a gorgeous ball gown the next. Because Ralph Nelson wasn't utilizing any magical effects, this was accomplished by a camera moving down to expose my dazzling shoes. The camera then gently zoomed back up while someone was busily pinning a new hairpiece and crown on my head and hanging a shawl around my shoulders. The change was complete by the time it reached my face. It was dangerous, especially on live TV. There were so many people working on me that I was attempting to stand still and accommodate them while still making it look acceptable and effortless for the cameras.

We recorded a cast album with a twenty-eight-piece orchestra for Columbia Records two days before the airdate, which was to be published the day following the transmission. I'm not sure how the albums could have been printed and ready that rapidly.

The lovely musical arrangements were created by Robert Russell Bennett, and it was thrilling to work with the man responsible not only for the arrangements for My Fair Lady, but also for the great spacious sound so evident on many Rodgers and Hammerstein shows—Oklahoma, South Pacific, and Carousel. The orchestra rehearsal was fantastic.

"You realize that possibly more people will see this show in one night than if you played in My Fair Lady for fifteen years," some "good friend" told me the night of the telecast, immediately before we aired. It wasn't quite what I needed to hear at the time.

Later, I learned that Cinderella had more viewers than any other show in television history. The evening went reasonably smoothly, and we all gave our best, but it felt a little imbalanced to me: too rushed, and lacking the seamless polish we could have had if filmed and polished for later viewing. It was very difficult work, but it was a tremendous learning experience. It took me years to comprehend the magnitude of what we accomplished that night.

My final Broadway performance in My Fair Lady was on February 1, 1958. Despite the fact that my contract in New York had expired, I had already promised to portray Eliza in the London production for another eighteen months. Rex and Stanley would also reprise their roles. We were supposed to start rehearsals on April 7.

As my contract came to an end, the Actors' Equity Association made a great deal about Anne being granted a work visa in the United States. Because of our connected paths in The Boy Friend, Tony and I were familiar with Annie. It turned out that one of the people causing the issue with Annie's visa was a British actor, although a U.S. resident, who was performing a minor role in My Fair Lady.

Charlie Tucker instructed me not to enter the United Kingdom until the first of April, when the new fiscal year began. Because I was in desperate need of a holiday, I planned to spend six weeks traveling through Europe, beginning in Paris.

Once My Fair Lady got on its feet, one of the first things I had to adjust to was a slightly altered pitch in the sound of our orchestra.

"Pitch" is the perceived basic frequency of sound, and our musicians seemed to play My Fair Lady's score with a slightly brighter, shinier resonance; not a different key, but a lifting of sound, possibly to give it more clarity. This could have been due to the acoustics in our venue, or it could have been because our conductor, Cyril Ornadel, favored that particular intonation.

The market was a bustle of activity back then, especially late at night when growers sold to shopkeepers, who then rushed the fresh items to their own premises in time for the morning shoppers. In 1974, the entire wholesale market was transferred to Nine Elms, and Covent Garden is now a highly posh neighborhood.

There was a little mirrored alcove in the room that had been transformed into a small bar, and I relished in watching my father take care of it, playing the grand squire—as if by instinct—when his guests arrived to attend the show.

The buzz surrounding My Fair Lady was incredible, and we all felt we couldn't possibly live up to it. The press was hailing the musical as the largest, finest, and most extraordinary ever to enter London, and we were afraid we were in for a surprise.

Tony and I entered the stage door at the conclusion of the evening well after midnight the night before we opened and were shocked to discover a large line of people going all the way around the theater, with bedding and chairs on the street. Tony and I stood and talked with them for a bit, and as we left, I expressed my hope that they enjoyed the show.

The following evening, April 30, my dressing room was so overflowing with flowers that I couldn't move. There was a gorgeous azalea plant bouquet from Charlie Tucker, but the most touching gift of all was a simple wooden Covent Garden flat tray loaded to the brim with bunches of dewy, fresh, sweet-smelling English violets— Eliza's flowers. My fortunate flowers.

When I opened the card, all it read was "With love from the opening night gallery queue." They had supposedly started a collection and purchased the violets from a Covent Garden seller. That gesture meant more to me than I can express.

The London premiere of My Fair Lady was more subdued than the Broadway premiere. The audience appeared a tad stodgy in comparison to the gallery throng. Noel Coward was present, as were many other celebrities, the majority of whom had attended the show in New York. Except for Donald and Chris, my entire family was present. Perhaps there weren't enough tickets available.

The show received mostly positive reviews, with only a few small quibbles. It may or may not be true, but I heard that the Daily Express critic criticized us in the first edition of the newspaper, and that Lord Beaverbrook, who owned the Express and loved the program, insisted on a favorable review. It was, indeed, by the second printing.

Her Majesty Queen Elizabeth and her husband Prince Philip attended a performance of My Fair Lady on May 5, which was far more elegant than the opening night, in my opinion. The royal box was decorated with flowers, and the theater was joyful. Our performance was outstanding. Following that, the Royals spent time with Alan, Moss, and Binkie Beaumont before returning backstage to welcome the cast. Her Majesty stated that she enjoyed the show, and Prince Philip lingered and chatted with Rex in particular. They must have spread their enthusiasm to other members of the Royal Family, because HRH Princess Margaret came to meet us on May 22.

When Sir Winston Churchill arrived to witness the show, we probably performed our most important performance. We all knew he was in the crowd, and we knew he wouldn't come backstage to say hello because he was elderly and in poor condition. He had asked for a copy of our screenplay, which he had read ahead of time. Our entire cast performed My Fair Lady for him and him alone—this remarkable man whom we adored, admired, and revered.

I recorded Rudolf Friml and Herbert Stothart's classic operetta Rose Marie with the magnificent baritone Giorgio Tozzi from July 22 to July 25. The New Symphony of London, conducted by the renowned Broadway conductor Lehman Engel, accompanied us. On Broadway, he conducted Fanny and Wonderful Town, as well as other Gilbert and Sullivan operettas. He was precise and skilled at what he did, and he assisted me in rising to the challenge of pure operetta. I thoroughly appreciated the entire experience. What amazes me is how I fit it into my hectic schedule. It's no surprise that I periodically had vocal issues.

She demonstrated how to work the stiff brush around the base of the wainscoting while on her hands and knees. She would pull all the dust and lint from the carpet's edges about a foot into the room with a swift flick of her wrist. She wiped down every top surface with the soft brush, including picture frames, entrances, shelves, and window casings. She vacuumed up whatever was on the floor and then used her soft duster to go over all the critical surfaces.

Sandy Wilson, of The Boy Friend fame, had asked Tony to design a production of Valmouth, a musical. His sets and costumes were stunning. He'd taken over our second bedroom and turned it into a workroom/study for himself. My attempts to keep that space tidy were increasingly useless as pads, pencils, inks, drawings, set models, memorabilia, and reference books filled every conceivable nook and corner. My father built some bookcases in our front hall for us, which helped a little. He also gave us a hand-turned wooden fruit bowl as a housewarming gift, which I still treasure.

DURING THE SUMMERThat summer, I met with the designers at Madame Tussaud's Wax Museum, who were creating a wax replica of me as Eliza Doolittle due to the success of My Fair Lady. Not only were photos of me taken, but also of my outfits, and I posed for comprehensive measurements of my entire body and face.

A gentleman arrived at our new flat with six lengthy, leather-bound jewel cases. With a flourish, he ripped open the lids, revealing pair after pair of glass eyes, all different hues and peering in all directions. He then held up one eyeball at a time, comparing it to mine.

I caught a nasty sickness and had to miss a couple performances of the musical. When I was recovering, I recall thinking that it was critical that I get back into shape; now was the time to be fitter than ever before. I resolved to engage in a strenuous workout.

I stretched, but clearly did not warm up enough, because when I moved on to the heavier exercises and attempted one that was really strenuous—a swing to the right, a swing to the left, and a swing all the way around—I hurled myself into it and threw my back out completely on the first rotation. I just couldn't move. I was scheduled to return to the event that night and wondered whether this was something I did unconsciously to avoid returning. I practically dragged myself to my bed and cried myself to sleep.

Dr. Walton arrived and helped me to my seat at his table. He helped me regain mobility with a long massage and a lot of manipulation. He'd never treated me before, but after looking at my back, he stated, "You know, you have a nasty curvature of the spine—a scoliosis." I'd never heard of it before. Dad W. believed it was most likely congenital. Thank goodness for his exceptional care, direction, and tuition about it, because it has continued to bother me in the years afterwards, and I've had to make allowances for it, such as particular stretching exercises and shoe changes. I returned to the concert after several days, therapies, and relaxing drugs.

Tony and I had kept in touch with the exquisite dancer Svetlana Beriosova while we were in New York. We received an invitation to her wedding reception after we returned to London.

We were eager to leave and were greeted by the groom, Mohammed Masud Raza Khan, whom we had never met before. He greeted us warmly and embraced me in his arms.

He was the affluent Pakistani landowner's son. He was tall and extremely attractive, with dark flashing eyes, a mustache, and a thick head of hair. He had a wide, somewhat sagging lower lip that was attractively pouty—perhaps a subtle clue of his cigarette addiction.

Sometimes he and Svetlana would get into a big fight, and Tony and I would calmly wait for them to calm down. Svetlana, who adored Sudi, would quarrel fiercely. Sudi was extraordinarily clever, but he wasn't always emotionally healthy, as I learned. His personality appeared to be split down the middle, as if he were completely trapped between eastern and western cultures; one half was the imperious son of a landowner, the other a well-trained London-based analyst, a disciple of D. W. Winnicott, the great psychoanalyst whose papers he eventually helped to edit.

In the years since his death, there has been much controversy about his working practices with his patients. His academic papers, on the other hand, are well regarded throughout the psychoanalytic community, and I'm very certain that he was a better thinker than a practical psychoanalysis.

Svetlana was caring and sweet, and her laughter was almost always present. She would supervise their houseboy's cooking and serving of plain meals at the table—mostly steak, veggies, and baked potatoes. She was everything I wanted to be: committed, disciplined, and with a strong work ethic. She seemed to have very few wants in life and limited her requirements to a bare minimum. She went to ballet classes every day; she never grumbled, never put on airs; and she was wonderfully beautiful with her Russian, triangular face. Everything she did reflected a strong sense of integrity.

We went to her performances whenever we could. The legendary Kenneth MacMillan, then a young, up-and-coming choreographer, composed several ballets for her. We saw her perform Giselle, Sleeping Beauty, and Swan Lake. She was always excellent, a little more intimidating than some dancers due to her height—and she was also a brilliant performer.

It was an exciting time for all of us. We were both part of London's young artistic community, and we were drawn to each other for a variety of reasons. There is no better way to spend an evening than to see a ballet performance at the Royal Opera House, followed by dinner at a restaurant or at Svetlana and Sudi's residence. We were frequently joined by other Royal Ballet dancers, as well as writers, analysts, actors, and directors, and we would speak about anything and everything till all hours.

Perhaps it was because the words were hers, or perhaps they were just delivered at the precise moment I was ready to hear them, but I became conscious of a newer, deeper meaning to my craft and what I was doing. I had always thought that my singing voice was a rare gift that should be treasured, but suddenly I felt that my entire body might be used to give something back—to express my thanks for the gift more thoroughly.

During my early years in vaudeville, most of my job was—well, work. That's what I did. And it never occurred to me in my childhood that when I appeared onstage, I might be able to make a small difference. I began to feel fulfilled in the act of doing—in the endeavor to express joy and pleasure to people; to assist them transcend their everyday troubles and problems for the short hours that they are a part of the theater experience. I was looking for reasons, motivations, a deeper core—and an explanation for why I had been given the gift in the first place. Whatever the inspiration, the brief conversation with Svetlana that day changed my life.

Chapter 8

When the flute calls and the trumpet answers, when voices are raised in practice and passages of song, when the Tannoy squeaks and disembodied instructions echo through the corridors, when the orchestra moves into the pit and the musicians check their pitch, there is a tingle of anticipation.

Most importantly, it is the music—when a big sweep of sound inspires you to try things you might not have considered feasible earlier in the day. When the orchestra swells to back your voice, when the music is perfect and the words are so beautiful that no one else could possibly say them, when a modulation occurs and raises you to an even higher plateau...it is ecstasy. And now is the time to share it.

My Fair Lady was recorded again at Abbey Road Studios in London in February 1959. The first Broadway album was recorded in monaural sound because that was all that existed at the time, then stereophonic sound arrived, and the record industry had to remake itself. It was critical that we record a new album for our show.

The English company went into the studios with, I suppose, a somewhat expanded orchestra—and I am so delighted we did. I believe Rex, Stanley, and I performed better on the second record. I'd settled into my role, I knew what I was doing, and while there are some things I wish I'd thought of adding, the stereo recording is light years better than the original, and it's the one that's officially used today.

Tony was putting in long hours. He was involved in four theatrical plays in London in 1959, and I enjoyed watching him construct and develop them. The first was a play called Fool's Paradise by Peter Coke, for which Tony did both sets and costumes. Cicely Courtneidge, an elderly actress, played the lead. Tony would return home from her outfit fittings, pleased and perplexed. "I don't understand it," he admitted. "I'm unable to properly fit her dresses." Every day, her stomach moves!"

Tony provided sets and costumes for the final play in 1959, a revue called Pieces of Eight. The majority of this revue was written by

99

Peter Cook and Harold Pinter, with a tune or two by Lionel Bart, subsequently of Oliver! fame. It starred Kenneth Williams, the extremely gay and humorous comic who is well-known among English audiences, and was directed and choreographed by a young man named Paddy Stone. I've collaborated with Paddy on various occasions throughout the years, most notably when he choreographed the films Victor/Victoria and S.O.B., in which he also appeared.

Tony and I agreed on May 10th as our wedding date. After a year with My Fair Lady in London, I was due for a two-week vacation in May, which coincided well with our plans.

Because of the spontaneous nature of our engagement, I never had an engagement ring, but Tony had given me a beautiful tiny brooch in the style of a laurel wreath while we were in New York, the same size as a ring. My wedding band had a similar laurel circle. Cartier manufactured it, and it was engraved on the inside.

Photographs of me in Eliza's flower girl costume were taken and displayed about his studio for him to study while he painted, but he also required multiple sittings with me. It was challenging to fit everything in because I was performing in the play, organizing the wedding, and having fittings for my gown.

Charlie Tucker was the owner of the portrait. It had been in his office for many years, but when he no longer represented me, he auctioned it off. I was married to my current husband, Blake, at the time, and he arranged for a buddy to go bid on it. I heard Charlie inquire whether this friend was bidding on my behalf, and he appeared pleased when this was confirmed. I am overjoyed to have it, and it now hangs in my home.

Rachelle was going to make my wedding gown, and she told us that the best material option might be obtained in Switzerland. We managed to squeeze in a quick trip to Zurich, where we selected a bolt of gorgeous white organza dotted with embroidered white roses. We also discovered some exquisite water silk taffeta, which was turned into a lovely evening gown for The Jack Benny Show. Tony created the outfits for the bridesmaids and maid of honor, which Rachelle also constructed.

Tony and I wanted to marry in St. Mary's Church in Oatlands, near Walton and Weybridge. The church is beautiful—the most beautiful in the neighborhood. Its lichen-covered gate is topped with a little V-shaped roof, and a country path leads up to the church doors.

We were introduced to the organist who would be playing during the ceremony on one occasion. He said that he owned "the finest organ in the south of England." Tony and I couldn't stop staring at each other, and we subsequently retold the event with delight.

Charlie Tucker was displeased that I was getting married. I believe he believed Tony wasn't old, intelligent, or affluent enough for me. Strange things began to happen, leaving me feeling a little nervous. I can't prove Charlie had anything to do with them, but I'm very sure he did.

I had lunch with the doctor on occasion. He was charismatic, elegant, and erudite, and he was Austrian. Our discussions covered a wide range of topics. He invited me to his office for our last interview, where I sat on one of his patients' couches. I recall crying a lot while telling him about my childhood. When the session was finished, he tenderly caressed my brow. Despite all of our gatherings, no articles were ever published.

He informed me he was going back to South Africa for business in a few days and wished he didn't have to leave. He stated that he would contact me. I received a lovely bouquet of tuberoses from him, and then I heard nothing more. My guess was that Tucker had asked him to soften my stance on marriage to Tony. Charlie's attempts to control every part of my life were becoming awkward, and while I was thankful to him, I became uneasy with his management style and the way he represented me. Despite Charlie's doubts, the wedding took place.

MAY 10, 1959 began bright and sunny. The night before the wedding, I stayed at The Meuse. For several weeks, I had been apprehensive, yet on this day, I felt peaceful and pleased.

Tony and I waited in line for a long time. Svetlana and Sudi, Zo, Charlie Tucker, Lou Wilson, Maggie Smith, Stanley, and Lainie Holloway were among the roughly 300 visitors. Toasts were made, and the cuisine was delectable. The multi-layered cake was cut and bits were kept for friends who were unable to attend. Speeches were given, both humorous and loving. There were photographs taken.

We remained at the Beverly Hills Hotel, where we met Bud Yorkin, the director of The Jack Benny Show. He was best known for directing the Emmy-winning Fred Astaire TV specials, which were both stylish and graceful.
Phil Silvers appeared on the show as a guest, and right before the special's conclusion, he said, "Julie. You're on vacation...I'd like to request a favor. "May I dance with the bride?" I asked, and we waltzed. He was a charming and hilarious man.

The music was pounding by the time we got past the massive bouncer at the front door and to our seats, and she was just finishing her first session, already completely naked. I'd never seen a stripper before. I had to sit down soon after seeing this lady dancing so erotically. We had a fantastic evening once I had my naiveté under control.

Tony and I were asked to a cocktail party at the home of our friend Edie Adams, who was now married to Ernie Kovacs. It was opulent, and the visitors included some of Hollywood's most powerful figures.

I recall seeing Jack Lemmon talking with filmmaker Blake Edwards, who seemed gorgeous and charismatic, though a little arrogant. I think I would have fainted if I had known that almost eleven years later I would be married to that remarkable gentleman. (I believe we all would!) But I was on my honeymoon with Tony, and Blake and I were only passing through the night.

The Jack Benny Hour aired on May 23, the same day Tony and I traveled back to England, so we missed it. The next day, I returned to My Fair Lady, and thus our married life started.

Although my contract in London was for eighteen months and I was supposed to leave the show in October 1959, I really left on August 8, two months early, because I was fatigued and as concerned about my voice as I could be.

It had been a marathon of two years in New York and sixteen months in London, not to add all the rehearsals and being out of town. I never knew if my voice or stamina would hold up on any given day. Most of the time, it did, but I was always a nervous wreck.

When I finished My Fair Lady, it was as if I had exited from a long, narrow tunnel into dazzling sunlight. The world had gone Cinemascope, and I had a life again. I had a lot of affection and care for the show, and I had a great send-off from the company...but the relief was enormous.

That show's experience will live on in my bones for the rest of my life. In the song "Just You Wait," Eliza imagines the King proclaiming, "Next week, on the 20th of May, I proclaim 'Liza Doolitle Day.'" Every year on May 20, I receive cards from friends and fans.

I'm frequently asked how I felt about not being cast as Eliza in the film adaptation of My Fair Lady. Alan had hoped that Warner Bros. would cast me, but the part was eventually awarded to Audrey Hepburn. I absolutely understood their decision at the moment. Warner Bros. required a huge name for the marquee, and while I had starred on Broadway, it was a pretty little pond in comparison to the rest of America and the rest of the world. In subsequent years, I wished I could have recorded my performance somehow, somewhere, for posterity—or at the very least for my grandchildren. Audrey and I became good friends, and one day she told me, "Julie, you should have played the part...yet I didn't have the guts to say no."

In late October 1959, I began work on The Julie Andrews Show, a four-part BBC programme. We would record one show per week. The director was Pauline Grant, the choreographer was Kenneth MacMillan, and Tony designed the sets. It was decided that in addition to singing and entertaining, I would do celebrity interviews. Vic Oliver, Richard "Mr. Pastry" Hearne, comic Kenneth Williams, and Pietro Annigoni were among my visitors.

We had heard that Mr. White was a recluse who lived on the isolated Channel Island of Alderney, and that he would probably not come to the mainland for anything so insignificant. Regardless, the offer was made, and to our surprise and happiness, he accepted. (When we asked him afterwards why he decided to appear, he claimed it was because he knew nothing about television and wanted to learn how the cameras worked and what went on set.)

Tony and I fell in love with this adorable, professorial man within days. He resembled Ernest Hemingway almost perfectly, albeit Tim was taller. His beard had turned yellow from smoking. He had fine white hair and wore generally corduroy and casual clothes, however he occasionally wore a stunning red bow tie.

He wandered onto our studio set and pottered around, and when it came time for the interview, he patiently put up with my asking him some very mundane things. I was anxious about doing interviews and wasn't very good at it. He appeared to be having a good time, and even if he wasn't, he wouldn't have indicated it. Tim had a personal code of honor that obliged him to treat everyone with the same decency as the medieval knights in his excellent book.

We ended up having four decent shows, the last of which aired on Christmas Eve. In December, I performed in a midnight gala at the Lyric Theatre on Shaftesbury Avenue to collect funds for the thousands of people affected by the Malpasset Dam collapse in Frejus, France. It was an all-star roster that included both American and British stars.

He sent me a modest bouquet of violets the next day, along with a letter written on a large piece of stationery with only two words each line.

"Dear Miss Andrews," it wrote in tiny handwriting, "I am so sorry for not introducing you correctly last night, but my car was towed away and I'm afraid I was not my usual self." Please take these flowers as my sincere apologies." The year finished with another Cinderella performance, but this time I was enjoying Prokofiev's ballet at the Royal Opera House, and Svetlana was dancing the main role. The evening was one to remember.

OF Something that had been niggling at the back of my mind came into focus around Christmas Time 1959. For a long time, I had been concerned about my brother Chris. My younger sibling was now more alone than ever, with Donald abroad in the merchant navy. The Meuse was run-down, with gloom in every room. Mum was away and spent most of her meals and evenings at the pub. The "local" had become her crutch, and the exquisite pianist who had formerly had such a fine technique was now merely a bar performer banging at the keys, her drinking buddies encouraging her lifestyle. Pop had a slew of occupations, first selling cash registers, then Hotpoint, and eventually Green-shield Stamps, so he wasn't around much. Aunt continued to teach after her divorce from Uncle Bill, although she eventually moved her school into the town hall and took lodgings for herself down the road. The studio at the back of our house, as well as the small bungalow, had fallen into disrepair.

Chris had taken a toll; he was now thirteen, pale, distant, and on the verge of a terrible depression, if not already there. I quickly knew that unless he got away, the conditions he was in would have a long-term impact on him.

In late January 1960, I returned to New York to film The Fabulous Fifties, a two-hour prime-time variety program for CBS that highlighted the decade's most popular theater, movies, books, and music. Even though Rex and I were no longer performing in My Fair Lady, we videotaped rehearsal sequences. I was shown practicing with Alfred Dixon, the dialogue coach who helped me perfect my cockney accent, before performing "Just You Wait." Rex performed a comedy on his first experience singing with an orchestra. The special won an Emmy for best variety programming.

The island was a mile and a half wide by three miles long, with huge cliffs at one end, heather, gorse bushes, cobblestone streets, and brightly painted stone houses on the flat end, and a charming port with a lighthouse on the flat end. The sea could be seen from practically every vantage point.

Because of its important location in the English Channel, it had been severely defended over the ages with Roman, Georgian, Victorian, and eventually German structures—forts, gunneries, bunkers, lookouts, and tunnels and storage vaults. The majority of the latter were now being gradually reclaimed by nature, with wild blackberries, nettles, grasses, and thistle covering them.

Tim was a true loner. Terence Hanbury White was born in Bombay, India, in 1906, and went to England with his parents when he was five years old. He had been a teacher and the head of the English department at Stowe, a prestigious boarding school in Buckinghamshire. After a few years, he retired and moved to a small house on the school grounds to pursue his writing and his passion for falconry. He penned the first volume of his epic work, The Once and Future King, there. He resided in Ireland for a while before relocating to Alderney in 1945.

Tim's house was actually two stone cottages combined, with a tiny rock garden in the back and a swimming pool. He told us that he had cleaned his house since a "great star" was going to stay with him (me!). It had recently been whitewashed, and he had fully redecorated it in a mini-Versailles style. There were new fixtures, throw rugs, and laundry baskets, as well as dazzling plastic chandeliers and wall sconces. He was extremely proud of his decorating abilities.

He appeared to enjoy having us around. He loved showing us across his world, driving us around and striding across fields and along beautiful beaches. He showed us the thirteen forts and castles built at strategic locations on the island, some rebuilt and privately owned, others in ruins. We investigated the German gun emplacements left over from the Nazi takeover of Europe during WWII. We went down a sheer hill to Telegraph Bay, a rocky beach.

Tony discovered some Dylan Thomas recordings and put "Do not go gentle into that good night" on the antique phonograph and set the volume up quite loud. There was a long hush after the poem ended. "PUT IT ON AGAIN!" yelled Tim, his voice choking. Tony played it again and again until Tim finally arrived downstairs.

Tim, I believe, was an unsatisfied gay who suffered greatly as a result. He drank a lot, usually Pernod, especially in the winter, but he was clean all summer for a purpose. He adored a young man, and he told us endless stories about him. Every summer, his parents permitted him to see Tim, and Tim relished the opportunity to teach the child how to fish, swim, sail, hawk, and read. I don't believe the relationship really ended, but the lad's parents were concerned, and he was eventually barred from seeing Tim. It crushed Tim's heart and turned him bitter.

We spent two weeks in Juan les Pins with the Waltons that summer. Mum and Dad W. rented an apartment on the promenade near the beach. Tony and I enjoyed a great time with them, swimming, sunning, shopping, and eating leisurely dinners at local restaurants.

We stayed in the South of France after they left, meeting Svetlana and Sudi in Monaco and spent the following two weeks at the magnificent Old Beach Hotel on the peninsula. The sound of the sea was steady and lovely because our circular room was right above the rocks facing the Mediterranean. We ate breakfast in our room and brewed tea in cups using one of those filaments that heated the water. One exploded in the bathroom one day, and I had to clean it up quickly before the hotel employees found out.

I sunbathed and napped to my heart's content. I tanned while lying on the beach. I would stretch out on my stomach and remove the back of my bikini top to avoid strap marks, and one day, after falling deep asleep, I was fully showered by a wave from the approaching tide, which was chillingly cold on my warm back. I screamed, only to find that my top was still laying on the ground.

It was a wonderful vacation, and I'm sure the carefree summer was one of the reasons I never missed a performance during my eighteen months in Camelot.

I drove down to Ockley just before leaving for New York to spend the day with Dad, Win, Johnny, and Shad. Dad was playing cricket for the home team on a Sunday. He was devoted to the game and played every weekend he could. He frequently expressed his desire for me to attend a match.

The family sat on the grass under a tree, Leith Hill in the background providing a wonderful backdrop for the village green and its velvet-smooth cricket pitch. We sat and spoke while watching the game, the afternoon heat, the click of the ball, and the occasional cry making one want to nod asleep. We all perked up when Dad emerged from the pavilion and headed onto the pitch. He looked gorgeous in his whites, and I'm sure he was aware of our presence and intended to play a respectable game. He did, indeed. The runs started to pile up: thirty—forty—would he make it to fifty? Johnny and I exchanged glances, both of us tense with anticipation and dread. Forty-eight, forty-nine—we held hands—and then there were fifty runs on the board. Dad, you're the best!

In late August, Tony and I left for New York. We traveled with Shy and landed in a bright, furnished apartment overlooking the East River. The view of the river, with tugs and cargo barges plowing up and down and the 59th Street Bridge nearby, was a welcome change from the dismal little ground-floor flat we occupied during My Fair Lady.

A great cast has been put together. Richard Burton, the charismatic stage and screen actor, played King Arthur. Lancelot was played by Robert Goulet, a Canadian rookie at the time with a great baritone voice. Roddy McDowall played the villainous Mordred, and Robert Coote played the clumsy King Pellinore. Though his role was little, Roddy had campaigned hard for it and would not back down, wanting to come aboard for the fun of it and to be among friends. John Cullum, who is now a star in his own right, was in the chorus, and Mel Dowd as Morgan Le Fay. Hanya Holm was once again our choreographer, Franz Allers was our maestro, and Abe Feder was our lighting designer. Our stage manager was a great gentleman named Robert Downing, who was supported by Bernie Hart. I was in the company of wonderful friends.

On September 3, 1960, rehearsals began in New York, and members of the company worked once more in the rooftop theater of the New Amsterdam on 42nd Street, while the principals rehearsed and blocked the show at the old 54th Street Theater.

As with My Fair Lady, I looked for omens as I drove to work that first day, and I saw a couple, so it appeared like everything was in our favor. Good!

Tony attended the read-through and was impressed, as was Richard's wife, Sybil. She was a gorgeous, small Welsh woman with a lovely countenance and a high chin. She exuded a carefree, outgoing demeanor. Roddy knew almost everyone in the room, and it was great to see him again. Robert Goulet, who was stunningly attractive, was probably as apprehensive as I was that first day, but he was immediately polite.

The distinct distinction between Act I and Act II became clear as rehearsals progressed. The drama opens on such a light note. The first scene is a mini-play in and of itself, and it is masterfully crafted. The first act has a joyful romantic atmosphere to it, but the second act sinks into darkness as it recounts the Round Table's collapse, and the show's ending is heartbreakingly tragic. This is the subject of Tim's wonderful book, but there was some concern that audiences would object to being led down one path only to discover themselves on another.

Richard, on the other hand, was having none of these issues. His singing was a revelation; those warm Welsh tones, polished by years of Shakespeare, gave him a vocal ease that was admirable. I completely melted the first time I heard him sing Alan's gorgeous ballad, "How to Handle a Woman," and there wasn't a night during the run when I didn't pause to admire his delivery of the subtle lines and lovely melody.

Abe Feder opted to use airport floodlights to mimic the splendor of the ancient Book of Hours to compliment Oliver Smith's stunning surroundings. When one walked onto the set and was blasted by another flood of light from the front, the consequence was a visual blackout. We couldn't see anything; there was such a haze of light that we actually had to look at our feet to gain our bearings, and we had to tread carefully. We grew accustomed to it over time.

On the show, Richard had a personal dresser who was a dear friend and had previously worked with him. Bob Wilson was his name. He was a handsome man, tall, quiet, tactful, and decent. He was well-versed in Richard's eccentricities. Sally, Bob's wife, was also a dresser, and because I, too, needed someone to assist me in the theater, it made perfect sense for everyone involved for her to come aboard and work for me. Sally was a lifesaver, a calming presence who kept my life in order.

Joyce Haber, a young lady from Time magazine, came to conduct a cover feature article on Lerner and Loewe. Although they had successfully developed the film musical Gigi in the interim, this was their first stage musical since My Fair Lady. There was a lot of speculation about whether they would hit gold again.

Joyce Haber was pleasant. She requested interviews with all of the principals, which she received, and she stayed with us for over two weeks to witness and document every minute of the out-of-town procedure. We opened our hearts and welcomed her into the company, led first and foremost by Richard.

Moss invited Richard and me, as well as Roddy, Mel Dowd, and Robert Coote, to his hotel suite after the event. He stated that he had been working on his memoirs and asked if we would listen to a few chapters. Wouldn't we?

We kept working hard in Toronto, practicing and adapting to Moss' edits virtually every day, in addition to doing our customary eight gigs a week. Franz Allers mercilessly drilled the orchestra and chorus, and the effects were evident. We all kept shaping our personalities and attempted to assist the potentially lovely musical find an easy rhythm and a cohesive whole.

Alan was sent to the hospital with internal bleeding caused by a perforated ulcer. It's odd that none of us were aware of his troubles at the time, despite Moss's knowledge. We were all pre occupied and preoccupied with the show.

Alan was standing near the hospital elevator on the day he was discharged when he noticed a patient on a gurney being pushed into the room he had just left. To his horror, he was informed that it was Moss who had died of a heart attack. It was catastrophic.

Moss's attack was not his first. He'd had one a few years before. He was going to be in the hospital for quite some time now. Moss's condition was not properly disclosed to the corporation. We were told he was in the hospital, and I guess we assumed he was suffering from the flu. We thought he'd be well enough to rejoin us when we arrived in Boston.

We had one more week in Toronto, and Alan made the sensible decision to allow himself and the company some breathing room. He let us play the extended version of Camelot for the rest of its run in the city and promised to continue working on it once we arrived in Boston. Meanwhile, the search for a director who could comprehend our current circumstances began, but the notion became unrealistic because the expectation was that Moss would soon be well enough to return to us.

After the production wrapped in Toronto, we relocated to Boston. We took a few days off while our massive sets were tracked down and crammed into the smaller area of the Shubert Theater. The principals were generally staying at the Ritz Hotel on the Common. Almost every evening, Richard threw a party in his suite. I believe he was lonely, and there were some regulars within the company who were only too happy to bolster him and drink with him every night, often into the small hours. Plus, of course, a lady or two to coo over him and hang on every word he says.

I'm pleased that Richard kept his cool with me and didn't try his luck until much later in the race. In all honesty, I'm not sure what my reaction would have been if he had put his considerable charms on me early in rehearsals. He was that appealing.

Chapter 9

Following the massive size of Toronto's O'Keefe Centre, Boston's Shubert seemed quite modest. We resumed rehearsals, working in the theater lobby or the bar downstairs while the setup and technical work onstage continued. Alan gave us additional cuts, and while Alan had to compose, his assistant, Bud Widney, practiced with us. We didn't see much of Fritz, and I subsequently learned that a serious schism was forming between him and Alan. Fortunately, we were all so preoccupied in the concert that we weren't aware of it.

Tony and Tim White were scheduled to return to New York from London. I'd been telling everyone about Time for a long time, and everyone was thrilled that he was coming to see us. I knew he'd be greeted and spoiled royally. It was agreed that Tim would not see the show until it was in proper working order, which might not be until our formal opening night at the Majestic in New York. However, Tony and Tim's jet was diverted to Boston's Logan Airport due to terrible weather on the very day we opened. Tony called to let me know he and Tim were going to be in town overnight.

I felt abandoned and quite alone after Tony and Tim went. I didn't want to be as gregarious as Richard, and I was tired. On a whim, I purchased a portable turntable and some beautiful recordings by Rachmaninoff, Brahms, Chopin, and Ravel. I found the music to be extremely pleasant and helpful in lessening my tension at the end of each day.

With no indication of progress from Moss, our opening in New York was delayed another week, and when we eventually arrived, we discovered that advance sales were strong, despite the fact that word had spread that we were plagued by troubles.

We had two paid previews in New York before our actual debut, and I received my song the night before the first one. It was called "Before I Gaze at You Again," and it was a lovely, straightforward song. Fritz had already planned everything, so I learned it, staged it quickly, and it went in that night. It holds a particular place in my heart.

Camelot premiered at the Majestic Theater in New York on Saturday, December 3, 1960. We limped into town and gave it our all for the show. Moss was unable to join us, despite the fact that he was now out of the hospital and recuperating at home.

The reviews were adequate but not outstanding. Camelot, in my opinion, would have had its own success if it had come before My

Fair Lady. As it happened, there were many unavoidable parallels to that big song.

Every critic had a different idea about what Camelot required. One person thought it should have been treated more "vastly," while another thought the unhappy conclusion should have been left out. The contrast between the behaviors seemed to bother or perplex most people. We appreciated the reviews to some level, but we were disappointed because, with all of our previous issues, we had never been able to perfect the show as much as it deserved. However, we never had a negative reaction from our audience.

The opening sequence of Camelot is a guaranteed thing to play. Arthur is upset because he has yet to see his bride-to-be, who is supposed to arrive at any moment. He climbs a tree and sees Guenevere fleeing her entourage, likewise displeased at being married off before she has had a chance to live. Arthur is taken with her, and they meet. He sings to her about Camelot's wonders, and his identity is revealed when his knights arrive to find him. Arthur tells how he extracted the sword Excalibur from the stone and thus became King. It's a fantastic speech, and Alan's words perfectly reflect the tone of the original book.

Goulet was so enamored with Richard's performance that he began to imitate it, augmenting his own character with a Shakespearean tone here and a flourish there. "I've suddenly become aware that Bob is doing my performance," Richard told me one day, "so I've had to change the whole thing." It wasn't exactly accurate, but it made for a fantastic narrative. In fact, I believe that through watching Richard, all of the knights in the play got a little grander, a little more noble.

Bobby Goulet had a fantastic singing voice, and his excellent looks made him the ideal of a true matinée idol. Every night, I would sit onstage as he sang to me, "If Ever I Would Leave You." He was dressed in a royal blue leotard, tights, and boots, and while I struggled to focus on my part, I found myself thinking, "My God! His legs are magnificent."

My Fair Lady was celebrating its fifth anniversary at the time, and Ed Sullivan chose to devote an entire hour of his legendary television show to Lerner and Loewe. After numerous songs from their earlier shows were played, a seventeen-minute clip from Camelot concluded the broadcast evening. This corresponded with the recent improvements to the show, and there was a real excitement that night. The next morning, there was a long queue of people waiting for tickets outside the theater and around the block. Camelot's sales skyrocketed, and it was finally a tremendous smash. It was a wonderful reward for our perseverance and hard work.

Despite the fact that the production was vastly improved, I believe it was never nearly the show it could have been. So many times after we had changed the play, members of the company would gather for a drink and someone would suggest, "Do you think if I did this here, it would help?" Or if I emphasized this line...?" I've never seen a corporation so enamored with a piece's potential. We were obsessed about it with Richard as our leader, and we had Time to thank for the magical book that started it all in the first place.

The last thing I thought about was what would happen to my voice when I stopped jogging and started singing. I flew onto the set one evening, managing everything flawlessly, opened my mouth to sing, and on the first intake of breath, something caught in my throat and I choked. I sang the entire tune, anxious to cough, tears welling up in my eyes, but I made it through.

That summer, my relatives came to visit. Dad and Win were the first to arrive, followed by Auntie and my mother. I had a great time showing them about the city, buying them performance tickets, and taking them on the boat tour around Manhattan.

It was so hot one night in New York that there was a power outage. The elevators in our building stopped working, so I had to walk down seventeen flights to catch a cab to the theater, and then climb back up when I got home. We had emergency power at the theater, but there were very few lights—we played basically in the dark, with no air conditioning, and were soaked wet within the first five minutes onstage in our medieval costumes. But the brave audience stayed with us the entire time, fanning themselves vigorously with their programs.

After almost nine months on the run, Richard began to act strangely. Ours had been a good relationship up until this point—easy, friendly, both of us sharing the stage with joy, providing support to each other. Our families were frequently social, and I never once sensed anything bad between us.

Tony claimed that our performances in Camelot were electrifying for about a week. I understand now that I was a fool not to put a stop to the foolishness. I should have asked Richard what he was doing. But I had a feeling something was up, which was verified by the next matinée when he knocked on my dressing room door. He was all smiles and gentleness, reaching out for a hug and asking whether I was okay. I then realized he was attempting to lure me into despair about his behavior. I believe I was the only lady in the company who hadn't succumbed to his allure—and perhaps this was meant to be my time.

Moss suffered another catastrophic heart attack on December 21, 1961, almost precisely a year after his second. He and Kitty were in Palm Springs, and a toothache, which always seemed to foreshadow Moss's attacks, had warned them of the likelihood of danger. He died quickly after collapsing in his driveway on his way to the hospital.

It was really devastating. He was only 57 years old at the time. Moss had attended the theater several times before I left for California, and one night he came to my dressing room and presented me with his own copy of Lady in the Dark. He asked whether I'd be interested in doing a new stage production of it, and I said I'd read it. As a fool, I thought it was a little dated. Gertrude Lawrence had starred in it with great success, but I was terrified and didn't believe Moss could pull it off again with me, despite the fact that he had asked me. I had not yet returned his copy of the play when he died, and when I finally asked Kitty if she wanted it back, she answered, "No, you keep it." I'd like to give it to you."

I was called back a few months later to join Carol on another Garry Moore Show. I completed four in total, three in 1961 and one in early 1962. In February 1962, I also taped a fantastic television spectacular called Lerner and Loewe's Broadway. It starred Bobby Goulet, Stanley Holloway, and Maurice Chevalier, and Richard Burton came over from Rome to perform the scene from Camelot's majestic Great Hall at the close of Act I. It was a beautiful and successful telecast.

Meanwhile, Lou Wilson's quick mind was working overtime. He and Bob Banner, who had some clout with CBS (they had funded both My Fair Lady and Camelot), came up with the wild idea that Carol and I should do a televised concert evening at the legendary Carnegie Hall. Putting two young musical comedy ladies in such a legitimate, classical setting seemed totally absurd, yet no one seemed to mind. Ken Welch returned to work. The majority of the production team from The Garry Moore Show, including Ernie Flatt, joined the show. The show was co-produced and directed by Joe Hamilton.

Carol and I were both familiar with Mike Nichols. Tony and I would occasionally go over to Mike's apartment and spend a quiet Sunday with him. For lunch, we'd bring smoked salmon and bagels, and Mike would concoct bullshots, a strong mix of bouillon and vodka. Mike would stretch out on his sofa while we spread out on the floor, listening to Callas, who was popular at the time, or talking about theater and reading all the Sunday papers.

On March 5, 1962, we filmed Julie and Carol in Carnegie Hall. We rehearsed on stage and blocked the day before, then taped a dress rehearsal the next day in case of mishaps, and performed the actual show to a sold-out audience in the evening.

Following an introduction number called "Together," we performed The Swiss Family Pratt, a parody of The Sound of Music. Carol played "Cynthia," the last kid and only girl in a family of twelve boys played by our outstanding dancers. It was a lot of fun, and I had no idea I'd subsequently be asked to play Maria in that magnificent picture.

Another musical skit in our act was inspired by the Russian dancing ensemble the Moiseyev—we renamed ourselves "The Nausiev." We also each sang a solo and collaborated on a massive twelve-minute medley of the decade's best tunes. At the end of the show, we replayed our "Big D" number, enlarged and upgraded to make it even better.

The choreography for the Pratt Family sketch on the Julie and Carol show called for Carol to "accidentally" strike me in the stomach, causing me to topple over. Carol was scared to think back on the moment she found out I was pregnant.

Of course, I gave Tony the wonderful news the same day. I wanted to broadcast it to the entire world. Tony was working on A Funny Thing Happened on the Way to the Forum's sets and costumes. It starred Zero Mostel, David Burns, Jack Gilford, and John Carradine. Tony was in the theater for rehearsals, and I dashed over to find him, but the first person I ran into was Stephen Sondheim, who was heading up the aisle. I told him my wonderful news. Tony still chastises me for telling Steve before I told him, but he always smiles, so I don't think he cared.

Camelot's final performance came on Saturday, April 14, 1962. Mum and Dad Walton were in New York at the time and attended the event.

I bid the company a fond farewell. Through the entire eighteen-month run, I had never missed a performance due to illness, and my faith in my capacity to survive the rigors of Broadway had been restored. I discovered what it felt like to be healthy now that my tonsils were no longer harming my system.

The following week, I spent nocturnal sessions with my pal Carol, recording Julie and Carol's CD at Carnegie Hall for Columbia Records. Then I went to Washington with Tony to watch A Funny Thing Happened on the Way to the Forum in previews. Forum is such a lovely, joyful show! It is still one of my six favorite musicals, along with West Side Story, Carousel, Guys and Dolls, Gypsy... and, of course, My Fair Lady. But those are just a few of my faves; I have many more.

Tony's creations were a riot of brilliant color. There was a brilliant, translucent crimson curtain in the show that was practically a hallmark of his work. Tony's favorite palettes are burnt oranges, reds, and corals, as well as midnight blues, aquamarines, and ocean colors. No one can match his unusual eye for combining tones, let alone his ability to create drawings that appear effortless and free.

It's a rare talent to make things appear so effortless that it betrays the dedication and hard work involved. Astaire possessed that, as did Rubinstein, Baryshnikov, Segovia, and certain painters, writers, and poets—those who transmit a sense of wasted strength and fire. It's an incredibly desirable trait.

The Forum premiered on Broadway on May 8 to rave reviews. Tony and I flew to California two days later, on our third wedding anniversary, to meet with Walt Disney, as planned.

On Mother's Day, Walt took us to Disneyland, which had been drawing huge numbers since its opening and was thriving.

experiencing Disneyland for the first time is an unforgettable experience, but experiencing it with Walt Disney as your guide was nothing short of spectacular. He and Lillian had their own private apartment overlooking Main Street's town center. It was a miniature recreation of a Victorian home, complete with a bedroom, kitchen, and offices that were all in perfect scale, furniture that was in proportion, and gorgeous fringed velvet lamps strategically placed throughout. Apparently, Lillian had intended it that way, and Walt had played along with her. They would occasionally assemble with the family there for a special function or gala evening, or possibly even stay overnight in the early days. It was never used by anyone else. It was the Disneys' personal retreat.

We were later welcomed back to the Disney home, where Walt had set up a tiny steam railway in the garden for his children and grandchildren. It was incredible to see the miniature railway line winding in and out of the flower beds and to hear the shriek of the little locomotive, which Walt enthusiastically drove. He always exuded the joy of a child.

We returned to the studios the day after Disneyland and listened to all of the wonderful songs for Mary Poppins composed by the Sherman brothers, Robert and Richard. The latter energetically played the piano. I detected a "rum-ti-tum" vaudeville quality in the tunes, and the significance of my early years in music hall clicked into place.

When Tony requested that he bring his portfolio to Hollywood, Walt took one look at it and signed him on the spot, commissioning him to design the film sets for Cherry Tree Lane and the interior of the Banks household, as well as all of the costumes, for which Tony received an Oscar nomination.

Walt had an uncanny ability to recognize genius in others. I think I should include the term "decency" as well. I never met a single person in his large organization who wasn't kind, eager, and generous. Everyone on the studio lot felt the Disney aura back then, and anyone who didn't have these attributes didn't last long. It was simple to express gratitude to Walt and accept his invitation to appear in the film.

We returned to London at the end of May. Alexa had left the United States the previous autumn. She'd taken Shy with her, dropping her off to our English vet's rural house to finish her quarantine and be mated again. We left Britain three weeks later for Alderney, where we spent a beautiful and glorious summer in our modest cottage. Though we had owned it for nearly a year, we hadn't yet claimed it as our own, and it felt like the ideal spot to spend my pregnant days.

I returned to the mainland on occasion for obstetrician visits and to interview prospective nannies, but for the most part, we spent the next two months cleaning, painting, buying furniture and necessities, and basically playing home on the island.

When we arrived at our new, tidy cottage, we discovered that the propane gas was not operating properly. The men fiddled with it, and I kept expecting them to blow us up. The prospect of the roast lamb I planned to cook on Sunday made me nervous. Having never prepared one before, I assumed it would take approximately nine hours to cook in our little and antiquated oven, which almost proved to be the case.

Tony and I lounged on remote beaches. I opened my growing tummy to the sky, believing that our baby would benefit from the fresh air and sunlight. My upper body suddenly had "une belle poitrine," and I had the bra size I'd always desired.

Tony has been asked to create two book jackets. He took over our modest dining table, and the stack of papers and doodles began to spread throughout the room. We passed the time by reading J. D. Salinger, making papier coupés, and writing stupid limericks.

Tim was anticipating company, and he was notorious for leaving things till the last minute. He stomped around grumpily, wondering who was going to put him in order. I'm not sure where kind Maisie was, but I marched down the lane to his house, armed with a pair of rubber gloves and one of my new aprons, and swept, dusted, shined, and cleaned his tiny kitchen and downstairs bathroom. Everything was covered in dust.

We, too, had a steady stream of guests, including Dad, Win, Johnny, Celia, Mum, Auntie, Donald and Chris, the Waltons, my old friend Sue Barker, and Sudi, to name a few. The latter was amusing, taking numerous images and cine film to share with Svetlana, who was working in London at the time. His voice rang out as he browsed in every store, apologizing to everyone he had inconvenienced. We had to stop every few seconds to show him our island, Sudi screaming out, "Julis!" Please exit the vehicle! Make a nice picture, talk to me, and say hello! Wave! That's all there is to it!" Stephen Sondheim visited for a short weekend, and we had a fantastic time together. I was concerned that Alderney was too barren, cold, and damp for him, but he declared that it matched his brooding attitude perfectly and that he couldn't be happier.

When Dad visited in August, we took part in Alderney Week festivities, going down to the village to see the three-legged race and the quoits tournament.

Summer went by in a flash. Tim began drinking again and became agitated and verbally unpleasant at times. He took Tony and me to supper at a posh restaurant on the island one evening. He insisted on having Jenny in the "No Dogs Allowed" dining room, despite the fact that we had left Shy in his car. He was so nasty to the waitress and in such a bad mood that I had to confront him. He stormed out of the restaurant before dessert, leaving little Shy to run around the parking lot and us to foot the bill and get a cab.

Emma and I did our first photo shoot with Zo just before Christmas. Who could have predicted that one of those images would find up on the cover of a tiny book Emma and I co-wrote forty-something years later?

Wendy, a sweet young nanny from Alderney whose parents operated one of the local hotels, was hired. Our apartment quickly became way too small. I recall being in the one and only restroom, which I now shared with Tony, Emma, and Wendy. Emma's clothing was hung on a plastic V-shaped washing stand in the bathtub. Under the sink was a massive diaper pail (no disposables back then!). The big pram was in the entrance, and Tony's artwork was still strewn everywhere.

Tony and I were exhausted from being awake every night with our hungry infant. We suffered for what seemed like an eternity, and one day, desperate, I contacted my mother.

My mother, who had raised four children, patiently explained that I was approaching the situation incorrectly. "By delaying her evening feed, she's getting her longest sleep before you even go to bed," she explained. "Wake her up every four hours, no matter what, and give her something to eat, and she will soon adjust to your schedule."

Emma was christened on February 24, 1963, at St. Mary's, Oatlands, the church where we were married. The Reverend Keeping did the honors, Emma behaved admirably, and all the Waltons, Wellses, and Andrewses met afterwards for a brief celebration at The Meuse. We left three days later for Hollywood.

Tony, Wendy, Emma, and I flew first class, seated on the front bulkhead. Emma flew pleasantly because the airline had positioned a bassinet against the wall.

I had not seen the house that Disney Studios had rented and equipped for us in Toluca Lake. When I first went to Broadway, I was once again entering a completely new universe. I had no idea that in the next few years, life would turn me inside out and upside down countless times. I only knew that everything was peaceful and joyful at the time, and I felt extremely fortunate. We were going to work together, we had a lovely infant daughter who was the love of our lives, and Walt Disney beckoned with gentle, creative hands.

As it happened...I was on my way home.

Printed in Great Britain
by Amazon

49894732R00069